GUILT AND REDEMPTION

Guilt
and Redemption

by

LEWIS JOSEPH SHERRILL

Revised Edition

John Knox Press
RICHMOND · VIRGINIA

Library of Congress Catalog Card Number: 56-13378

Revised edition 1957
Third printing 1963

To

PRESIDENT FRANK HILL CALDWELL
and
FANNIE WELLS CALDWELL

PREFACE

THE MATERIAL which follows was delivered, in substance and somewhat condensed, as the Sprunt Lectures at Union Theological Seminary, Richmond, Virginia, in February of 1945. No one who has had the honor of giving the lectures on this Foundation can ever forget the gracious hospitality extended by this Seminary to its guests, and the stimulating attentiveness with which a speaker's thought is met. In no way forgetful of numerous acts of hospitality and thoughtfulness extended by other persons to Mrs. Sherrill and myself, we wish especially to thank President and Mrs. Benjamin R. Lacy, Jr., and Professor and Mrs. W. Taliaferro Thompson.

These lectures spring from the conviction, growing steadily with each year, that Christianity has the most penetrating and the most constructive solution ever offered for the tremendous problems arising out of human guilt. But with that conviction has grown another also, namely, that Christians of our own day commonly are trying to use the resources of the Christian gospel and the Christian church without facing the depths of the guilt from which that gospel promises to redeem us. The redemption that is then realized among us is superficial and often even trivial, since the conception of guilt is not radical. That conception of guilt as expressed in historic Christianity is indeed radical, but the time seems to have come again, as it often has done previously in Christianity, when the vocabulary of religion serves to help us hide our faces from an understanding of the deeper meanings of sin.

Because of such convictions I have sought in these lectures to draw not only upon the Bible and theology, but also upon psychology and psychiatry. The latter two fields, so significant in modern life, are in no way substitutes for religion, but they hold promise of aiding us in utilizing more fully certain religious resources which, at the present, lie almost dormant within Christianity.

The preparation of this material has been to me a unique experience, so rich in comradeship that I cannot forbear referring to it, deeply personal though it is. When the invitation to give these lectures came, eyesight had been impaired to the point where reading was no longer possible. Learning of the invitation, friends in the community, associates in the institution of which I am part, and above all my wife, put at my disposal their time, their skills, and their specialized knowledge. So generous have they been that at the time the lectures were delivered, and now again as the book is published, I feel it would be both ungracious and untrue to present this volume as if it were the work of one person alone.

For the reading aloud of material needed in the writing, I am indebted to Mrs. Frank H. Caldwell, Mrs. Emmet F. Horine, Mrs. Sam W. Eskew, Mrs. Henry Sweets, Jr.; to Professors William A. Benfield, Jr., Julian Price Love, Walter A. Groves, and William D. Chamberlain; and to my daughter, Mrs. Hugh Murrey Durham. I wish also to thank the Rev. James W. Averitt for a service of lasting value.

Their competence in the fields of Bible and theology has made it especially valuable to have the suggestions of my colleagues in the faculty, when I attempt to draw upon those areas. President Frank H. Caldwell and Professors Julian Price Love, William D. Chamberlain, and Walter A. Groves have read parts or all of the manuscript and have shared their specialized knowledge unstintingly. Whatever errors in fact or insight may remain, for which I alone am responsible, I am sure these are much less numerous than would have been the case without these friends.

Because of their competence as psychiatrists, I have counted it fortunate that I could repeatedly discuss some of the issues approached in this book, with Spafford Ackerly, M. D., of Louisville, and with Carl A. Whitaker, M. D., formerly of Louisville, and now of Oak Ridge, Tennessee. As Director of the Mental Hygiene Clinic of Louisville, Dr. Ackerly, with characteristic generosity, gave permission to use such material in the following pages as comes from the records and the experience of that clinic. The cases, of course, have been disguised so as to prevent identification. Dr. Whitaker was for some years on the staff of the same clinic and during that period held conferences for several successive years with students of this institution, as has also been the case in previous years with Dr. Ackerly. To both these psychiatrists, several generations of students and I owe deep obligation which we gratefully acknowledge. Both psychiatrists have read this manuscript and have made suggestions which, I trust, have been incorporated in ways that are fair to them. With these psychiatrists, as with my colleagues in the faculty, they are in no way responsible for any opinions expressed or any statements made in this volume.

My secretary, Janice H. Moore, has rendered invaluable assistance by reading, gathering material, making digests, investigating special topics, preparing the material both for delivery and for publication, and seeing the book through the press. I cannot thank her sufficiently for help in finding ways of surmounting obstacles.

My wife, Helen Hardwicke Sherrill, is a psychiatric social worker on the staff of the Mental Hygiene Clinic of Louisville. Her familiarity with clinical experience and records, her library research, her discussions of these subjects with others, and her reading, all given without limit, have brought into this work as a whole elements which otherwise could not have been present. Our rich store of shared joys has been enlarged yet again as we worked together, and sought to penetrate further into the meanings which are in Christianity and in the healing forces of our universe.

· · · · ·

Permission to quote copyrighted material has been cordially given by Harcourt, Brace & Co., Oxford University Press, and The Westminster Press. Acknowledgment of this courtesy is made here, and in each instance of such quotations, further specific acknowledgment is made in the Notes.

L. J. SHERRILL

Louisville Presbyterian Theological Seminary
Louisville, Kentucky
April, 1945

PREFACE TO THE REVISED EDITION

In this second edition of *Guilt and Redemption* most of the text has been left unchanged. Some revision has been made in Chapter II where two major streams of psychological thought are distinguished and in Chapter IV where different kinds of anxiety are discussed.

LEWIS J. SHERRILL

Union Theological Seminary
New York, N. Y.
May, 1956

CONTENTS

⤞ I ⤝

WHERE IS THE BATTLEGROUND?

GUILT AND REDEMPTION have become strangely separated in modern life, with fateful consequences. They are separated as human experiences, as objects of thought, and as fields of specialized professional endeavor.

View the separation first in regard to redemption. In theology, in preaching, and in pastoral care, redemption has to do with sin and sinners. But redemption as commonly presented is something abstracted from life as ordinary people know it. Having little or no sense of guilt in a recognized form, they naturally conclude that "sin" is a matter with which "I" have no concern. What interest, then, can I possibly have in redemption? Let professional religious people work with the idea if they wish, but what personal stake have I in their jargon? So reason common people—perhaps —if they so much as give it a thought.

And guilt? We do not get rid of it merely by failing to recognize its existence or by misunderstanding its nature. It continues to be one of the common experiences, perhaps not of all persons, but certainly of many. By some it is overpoweringly felt, by others it is carefully hidden, and therefore may be disavowed too vehemently, or it may be cast on a scapegoat. Of these and many other forms which it takes we are yet to speak. But not infrequently it keeps on working its devastation even though cloaked with a fervent religious vocabulary. Suffering from some of its forms we go to physicians, grateful that someone in modern civilization is prepared to deal, partially at least, with crushing guilt. Suffering from other forms of it we go to war: war with those of our own household, war with the next door neighbor, war with the haves or the have-nots according to our hates, war with other nations, or war against war.

Can redemption and guilt be reunited in human experience? It is a daring hope, for the chasm now dividing them is deep. The habits of thought in much theology have grown so remote from felt reality as to make it seem now almost a heresy to turn theology toward guilt as it is actually experienced in modern life. And as for the guilty themselves, hopeless, or defiant, or hostile, they have learned the bitterest lesson which modern Christianity teaches, namely, that it has a remarkable metaphysical theory of redemption which in practice, in the hands of many of its servants, cannot reach down into the recesses of the human soul and set that soul free from guilt.

It is hoped, nevertheless, that these lectures may have some part in reuniting lines of thought which have been sundered quite unnecessarily; and, ultimately of far greater importance, that they may make some contribution toward ending the personal discontinuity between guilt and redemption in experience.

In such an undertaking we seem compelled to take our start with a consideration of guilt itself as a part of human experience, and to spend a substantial part of our time there. We shall not stop with that; on the contrary, we shall seek to put under tribute whatever in Christianity appears to have bearing on guilt. But we shall not begin at this latter point, for to do so involves the risk of repeating the very thing we wish to avoid, that is, abstracting redemption from actual life. This latter approach usually begins by setting up a theological dogma concerning human nature, and then one is able to show that his theory of redemption fits the alleged facts of human experience. In proportion as this is done, theology tends to create a picture of human nature which human beings themselves fail to recognize, with the consequence to which we have already alluded, that the proffered redemption seems alien and unreal.

But if we begin by considering guilt itself as a fact in human experience, we must be clear regarding one thing: we have not thereby necessarily shaken loose from dogma. For if we turn to psychology for data concerning human nature, we shall find the various psychologies just as heavy with dogma as any theological system. If dogma is statements pronounced true apart from evidence which any other competent person can verify for himself, theology and psychology are simply pot and kettle, neither having any ground to call the other black.

How then can we avoid dogma in psychology? It can never be done completely, and it is as well to be clear about that from the beginning. But two methods should aid us in steering away from authoritarian pronouncements in psychology. One is to use clinical material freely. Clinical material of course includes that coming out in the clinic properly so-called; but by a freer use of the term it may legitimately also take in facts concerning human nature as revealed by human beings themselves in whatever setting, religious or secular, public or private, ancient or modern. Much of the material will not even wear the name of "psychology," for much psychology stubbornly hides its face from reality, just as truly as much theology does; that reality meanwhile continuing to be revealed elsewhere to any who have the eyes to see it. Human living itself, that is to say, is a "clinic," or perhaps better a "laboratory," turning up its data which are essentially timeless. In this broad sense the clinic includes all known acting and thinking.

The other method which promises a measure of assistance in keeping free of psychological dogma, is that when dogma enters the picture it should frankly be labeled as such. At times this is easy, as when one can say that a particular proposition is a Jungian or a Freudian theory, as distinguished from clinical facts reported by a worker who happens to be a disciple of Jung or Freud. At other times separating dogma from clinical event will be far from simple, because we shall find ourselves involved in some modern belief so generally held as to make it almost impossible to distinguish dogma from event.

As soon as we begin the consideration of guilt we are confronted by a strange anomaly. On the one hand there has never been a time of such violence to life and property as we have witnessed between 1914 and the present, some thirty years at this writing; and the end is not yet in sight. Take the period alone of the less than five years that elapsed between September of 1939 and the spring of 1944. The roughest estimates of the human lives sacrificed in that span of time place Russian losses at fifteen millions, to say nothing as definite concerning the Chinese, the Germans, the Japanese, the Jews, the Poles, the French, the Greeks, the British, the Americans, and the others. The economic costs have been guessed at 600 billion dollars, in terms of armament and destruction. Now if guilt has any relation to suffering and losses caused, it might be supposed that the burden of guilt would destroy surviving aggressors and victors alike.

But on the other hand, in the midst of this actual destruction guilt seems seldom to enter as a recognized experience, except by way of charges which we hurl at others concerning their guilt.

There is a broad sense in which it can be said that we have disavowed both the concept and the experience of personal guilt for public happenings in modern life, and have placed responsibility on vague entities such as the State, economic conditions, international relations, war, and the like. The disarming naturalness with which we do this may, in fact, be but the first form in which one encounters a modern dogma concerning guilt. How far is the individual responsible for, guilty of, such phenomena as wars and depressions? The difficulty of such a question, our perplexity when we honestly face it, and the remarkable ease with which we side-step it, should, we suggest, put us in a more hospitable frame of mind toward a fundamental issue underlying the problem of guilt, an issue to which we may now direct attention.

WHERE IS THE BASIC CONFLICT?

The issue may be put most simply in the form of this question: Where or what is the seat of the basic conflict out of which man's sufferings arise?

That there *is* conflict any child soon learns, and every man has known from the dawn of human life, has known because it confronted him wherever he turned, has known because he could not escape it though he might fly to the ends of the earth. There is conflict in nature, as between cold and heat, day and night, storm and calm, beast and prey, conflict constantly symbolized in man's presence by the flashing stab of lightning and the angry roar of thunder. There is conflict between persons, ranging from the mildest disagreement between any two individuals to the fiercest warfare when virtually the whole of mankind are arrayed in two opposing camps. And there is conflict within the self, symbolized in an almost endless variety of ways, as when Goethe makes Faust say,

> "Two souls, alas! are lodg'd within my breast,
> Which struggle there for undivided reign:
> One to the world, with obstinate desire,
> And closely-cleaving organs, still adheres;
> Above the mist, the other doth aspire,
> With sacred vehemence, to purer spheres."[1]

Or as it is expressed in more homely words by a little clerk in one of Chekov's plays, "I am a man of cultivation; I have studied various remarkable books, but I cannot fathom the direction of my preferences; do I want to live or do I want to shoot myself, so to speak? But in order to be ready for all contingencies, I always carry a revolver in my pocket."[2]

But what is the nature of this conflict? Is there some ultimate issue, in terms of which the basic conflict or conflicts of existence can be stated? If so, it is to be supposed that individual life will orient itself to no small degree around the answer accepted as true. As will presently be shown, questions concerning the basic nature and meaning of the conflict in the universe have pressed in upon man's thought from a time so remote that all dates can be only the roughest conjectures. The answers proposed during a period of some four or five thousand years, at least, constitute a vast body of material coming up out of the clinic of living. The answers, or solutions proposed and acted upon, while inevitably different in numerous particulars, can readily be grouped in classes, and within these classes show a deep and striking kinship, regardless of the time and place in which they may be identified.

One such body of material comes from the remote past, consisting of man's early religious and philosophical thought, and will be examined in this lecture. Another comes out of present or very recent times, comprising man's self-conscious attempt to understand himself and his kind by means of psychology; this will be considered in the second lecture. Obviously each of these is so great in the extent of its material as to prevent anything more than pointers toward some of its meanings.

ANCIENT RELIGIONS AND PHILOSOPHIES

In examining material presented by man's early thought upon the ultimate issues of existence, we are plunged at once into a sea of mythology, as well as into bodies of philosophy some of which are so profound as to be a marvel to men of the present day. We shall shun no mythology from any quarter if it seems relevant, no matter how grotesque it may appear to our habits of thinking; for in the myths concerning the gods and superior beings we often have valuable, though indirect, evidence as to what man thought of *himself*, that is, of his own nature and his own relations to the universe as he perceived it.

As soon as one begins to examine this material, it becomes apparent that from the earliest known eras mankind itself has been divided over the location of the basic conflicts of human existence. To put the problem in its sharpest form immediately, is responsibility for suffering and evil finally within individual man himself, or is it somewhere outside of individual man, or is it perhaps some combination of these?

THE CONFLICT EXTERNALIZED

There is one great body of ideas which places the ultimate responsibility outside of individual man. The final conflict is thus put out beyond the self, and the self is then more or less clearly made a victim who is unable to explain his personal fate. The specific forms which this general sequence of ideas takes are as varied as the cultures out of which they sprang. We may refer briefly to a few of them, and take one for a slightly more complete consideration.

The Babylonian mythology illustrates a part of this sequence of ideas, at least so far as to show that conflict first arose among the gods. The account as the tablets have survived is badly mutilated, but enough is clear to give the outline of the account. Apsu was the primeval being. Mummu was the vizier of Apsu, and Tiamat was the mother of all the gods. Confusion soon arose among them; the way of the gods was not good, and Apsu determined to destroy them. But Tiamat, hearing of this resolve, went into a terrible rage, and planned evil in her heart. This tablet is incomplete, but apparently there was much disturbance among the gods because of rivalry and hostility. Apsu himself, the primeval being, was laid waste. Tiamat raises a war cry among the gods; they devise mischief day and night, and organize battle. Tiamat then engages in long and violent conflict until she, too, is destroyed. Marduk gains the ascendancy, becoming lord of the gods. He creates the universe out of the parts of Tiamat, whom he has dismembered, and then creates man. Thus the primal beings are destroyed, and the universe is brought into being by one who himself is a rebel.[3]

Early Vedic religion suggests, if it does not explicitly state, conflict within the Sun God himself, who is the supreme being. This god has five different names, representing as many distinct characteristics or qualities, which apparently could not be reconciled into one conception.[4]

This suggestion is worked out more explicitly in Brahmanism, which was an outgrowth of Vedic religion. Here both the gods and the evil spirits are born of the same Father-god. The gods are spirits of light, and the evil spirits or Asuras are spirits of darkness, with the result that light and darkness are arrayed against each other, as so often in religious symbols; but in this instance they both come from the same ultimate source. There is the significant further conception of conflict as seen in the belief that these beings inherit different aspects of the Father-god's nature; the gods inherit mind, while the Asuras inherit speech.[5] The consequence is that in the spiritual order of being, reason and expression of thought are separated; and man is, in one manner of viewing it, at the mercy of a sort of schizophrenic deity.

Among the American Indians there were myths attributing the conflicts which affect man, to sources outside of individual man. It is impossible to determine the antiquity of these beliefs, or to know how far they may reflect the influence of Biblical ideas which they may have absorbed. But in any event they seem to show essentially the same conceptions as those which we have just seen in the East.

The Choctaws believed that the world is peopled by two kinds of spirits, the good and the bad. These spirits are continually at war over man. The good spirits direct all things for his prosperity and happiness, while the bad spirits direct all things against him. Man himself can do nothing in the face of this contest over him, but must await its outcome.[6]

The Pueblo Indians of Acoma have a myth to the effect that the first creatures born were two female human beings. Their birth took place under the ground, and they lived long in this dark abode, being cared for and taught by Tsichtinako, the Thought-Woman. At last they emerged into the light, and each was provided with a basket containing seeds and a pair of images of every kind of animal. The sisters planted and nourished life on the earth. An evil spirit entered in the form of a serpent which dropped from their basket, grew, and tempted the sisters to reproduce themselves. They had been warned by Tsichtinako, the Thought-Woman, against reproduction, but nevertheless one of the sisters conceived and bore twin sons, whereupon Tsichtinako in anger forsook the sisters, leaving them to do as they saw fit.[7]

The Natchez Indians saw their world inhabited by good and evil spirits, having differing degrees of power in each instance. The greatest of the evil spirits had wrought such damage in the earth that the supreme good spirit, weary of the former's deeds, had caught and tied him, with the result that the evil spirit no longer had such power as formerly.[8] But this evil spirit was not vanquished; he was merely brought under a measure of control.

Formulations such as these shade almost imperceptibly into another group of ideas which still attribute conflict to sources outside of man, but which see man, either socially or individually, as a battleground for the same forces as those that contend against each other in the outer universe.

Aztec religion is a case in point. The Aztec saw a duality running through the entire universe. He witnessed struggle near at hand, but this was at least symbolical of, or perhaps partook of, the same conflict which he beheld everywhere. His ritual and his philosophy were permeated by a Sacred War which was being waged wherever he looked. The great gods of the sky were in battle with each other—light against darkness, heat against cold, rising sun against setting sun. Even stars grouped into contending armies of the east and the west. Gladiatorial combat between the great warrior orders, the Eagle Knights and the Ocelot Knights, symbolized this universal conflict.[9]

In Chinese thought, also, there is a duality which reaches into numerous aspects of existence. This duality is seen in the negative and positive principles of universal life, going under the name of Yin and Yang, respectively. Originally these words meant the dark and bright sides of a sunlit bank. By the time of Confucius (551-479 B. C.) they had begun to take on a philosophical significance, and have grown since in the importance of their application to human thought and affairs.

Yin and Yang themselves are held to have proceeded from some great ultimate. Yang is the positive principle, and represents heaven, light, warmth, vigor, productivity, the male, penetration, life, and so on. Yin, the negative principle, represents earth, darkness, cold, the female, absorption, quiescence, death, and so forth. The Yang is subdivided into a vast number of good souls or spirits called *shen*, and similarly the Yin is subdivided into a host of evil spirits known as *kwei*. These *shen* and *kwei* indwell every animate being and every thing. Thus every soul of man not only has its *shen* and *kwei*, but different aspects of the self are identified with one or the other; for example, the *shen* constitutes his intellect and his virtues, while the *kwei* constitutes his passions and his vices. In such a manner the duality of the universe itself is reproduced in every individual self.[10]

The duality seen by the Aztecs and the Chinese is also seen in a comparable form by the Zoroastrians. To them the whole world is a battlefield on which hostile forces contend without ceasing. One of these is represented by Ahura Mazda and his Kingdom of Light. Ahura Mazda is absolutely good, and as such cannot be the author of any sort of evil, physical or moral. The opposing force is represented by Angra Mainyu and his Kingdom of Darkness. All evils are the results of this being's power. Man is not a passive spectator of this conflict, for he himself is a battlefield for contending forces. Life and death are set before him, and in the judgment Ahura Mazda will reward a man according to the teaching which he has followed.[11]

Greek thought offers an excellent opportunity to examine what happened in the case of a people who placed the responsibility for man's situation in the laps of the gods.

Recorded Greek thought may fairly be said to have taken its start from the inquiry into the nature and origin of evil and suffering. Later, to be sure, this attempt was transformed into an inquiry into the nature of the good; but this was a riper product, and one that began because the limits of the earlier quest had been reached.

Many Greek minds were almost obsessed by man's plight, especially that of the person who had done no intentional wrong and yet was overtaken by sufferings beyond all human endurance. This is illustrated in Homer, Hesiod, the great tragedists, and to an extent also by the greatest philosophers.

The *Iliad* begins with the account of a pestilence that raged in the Grecian armies. The question is, why? Its cause is traced to the transgression of one man. The gods must be appeased for this sin— that much is taken for granted, and sacrifice is made.

But appeasing the gods for one sin did not get to the root of the matter; for the hostility of Agamemnon and Achilles toward each other flamed into the open, and why was that hostility between great men so bitter? The cause lay ultimately in the fact that the gods themselves were in conflict. Human beings thus did not originate their own crucial acts, but were only pawns pushed about by contending gods. Thetis took the side of the Trojans, and Hera was partisan of the Greeks. Zeus, ruler and arbiter of the gods, was of uncertain mind himself over the issue, and consented to a deception by means of which the Trojans broke their plighted word, a stratagem which outraged the moral sense of mortals, for all it had the power of heaven behind it. So when the final word was said, the conflict was first between the gods themselves, while men, impelled by divine decrees they could neither withstand nor understand, fell like flies before the pestilence or slaughtered each other in battle to satisfy the whims of gods who possessed all power and lacked moral standards.

Hesiod likewise sees this conflict and relates its origin to the gods in two distinct ways. In his *Works and Days* he begins with the proposition that two Strifes exist, of wholly different nature. The one, cruel in character, fosters evil war, lies and sorrows, quarrels and famine. The other, more kindly, stirs man to labor and to emulate the good neighbor. This much is hardly more than a recognition, so common in human thought, that there is some kind of cleavage in human nature itself. But with Hesiod the rub is that while the good Strife is descended from the gods, the gods themselves demand honor for the evil Strife.

So Hesiod pushes his inquiry still further, to ask how this conflict ever came to exist among the gods. The *Theogony* gives his second answer, in which there is the revealing clue that Earth, "the ever-sure foundation of all," is the mother of Heaven.[12] The first being of all was Chaos, next Earth, then Eros (Love). Earth bore Heaven, and Heaven in turn, mating with Earth, was the father and she the mother of the gods. The youngest of the gods was Cronos, who "hated his lusty sire."

Earth and Heaven mated again, this time bringing forth three "presumptuous children," stubborn and irresistible, "hated by their father from the first." These were stirred by Earth to revolt against their father, and taking a great scythe, they mowed off part of the father's body, leaving him maimed. So was the human situation projected into the race of the superior beings. And with human passions put into the pantheon, human woe was seen not merely as reinforced by, but springing directly from, the will of the gods.

Greek religion seemed wholly unable to break out of this circle, so much so that since Nietzsche it has become a commonplace to say that the religion itself is grounded in the conflict between two contending forces existing among the gods themselves. One of these is identified sometimes with Zeus and sometimes with Apollo, but in either case it points to such principles as law, order, justice, and reason.

The other is of a wild, unbridled sort, identified with Dionysus.[13] The latter originally was a rural god, who became associated with spring as his peculiar season, and with the reproductive forces of

nature. He was the god of the vineyard. The poetry and music
which he inspired were free and irregular, while the mood of response to him was that of gaiety, enthusiasm, and passion. His train
was made up of the Satyrs, a cowardly, sensual, lively, and humorous
race; of the Bacchanalians, the Centaurs, and Pan. An untrammeled
crew they were; but these were gods, as truly as were Zeus and
Apollo.

How, then, was man to bear his lot and live worthily when dominated by the gods and when the gods themselves represented such
conflicting forces? The great Greek tragedists take up the question.

A large part of the mass of material produced by these men is
occupied with the legends surrounding Agamemnon and his family.
Free as the tragedists were to manipulate the details of the story,
they kept remarkably close to great issues in living, and they recount
the surge of powerful emotions with a skill never surpassed.

One story with which they worked in a number of tragedies has
many variant details, but its thread is this. Agamemnon, king of the
Greeks, is husband of Clytemnestra, and his brother is Menelaus,
husband of that famed Helen who fled with Paris to Troy. To
avenge the insult, the Greeks assemble their ships and prepare to
sail against Troy. But the fleet is becalmed, and Agamemnon is in-
formed by a diviner that favorable winds will not blow until
Agamemnon has sacrificed his daughter Iphigenia. Clytemnestra,
hearing that her husband is preparing to appease the gods by this
gift of their own daughter, is overcome with horror. The apparent
conflict is between Agamemnon and Clytemnestra, husband and
wife, standing for the respective demands of state and family, race
and blood. As the conflict grows in its terrible strength and seems to
admit of no solution, Iphigenia, young girl that she is, rises to moral
grandeur, and freely offers herself for the welfare of Greece. But in
the background hover the yet more terrible gods, who exact such

sufferings from men, and who can be moved only by the immolation of a chieftain's daughter. And in Clytemnestra, the wife, there rises a hatred of her husband which knows no limits.[14]

Meantime the Trojan campaign drags on year after year, and Clytemnestra, left at home and hating her husband, yields to the whisperings of Aegisthus, who becomes her lover. The pair intrigue against Agamemnon, and when he returns victorious from Troy at last, it is only to be slain by his wife.[15]

But the tale of human passion, god-inspired, is to be still further unrolled. For besides Iphigenia, Agamemnon and Clytemnestra have two other children—a daughter Electra, and a son Orestes. Because of what Clytemnestra has done in murdering Agamemnon, Electra is enraged against her mother, and pours out such a torrent of hatred as is scarcely to be found elsewhere in any literature.[16]

But Orestes, the son, of stronger will, slays his mother. And for this, the Furies will not be appeased. He was incited to the murder by Apollo, yet the Furies pursue him, haunt him. And now it seems as if the powers of the unseen world are drawn up in array for Orestes and against him. Apollo is his defender, but to stir the heavenly feud to still greater intensity, the ghost of Clytemnestra spurs the Furies on. Orestes flees to the temple at Athens, a hunted wretch, Apollo protecting, the Furies defying Apollo and Athena, chanting their hymn of vengeance.

And then comes again one of those twists by which the Greek came back to earth; to solve the conflict, Orestes is put on trial before the burghers of Athens. In reality, it is the gods who are on trial before a jury of men! Apollo pleads that he has incited the deed only at the bidding of Zeus himself. The Furies howl for vengeance. The jury's vote is a tie. Athena breaks the tie, acquitting Orestes. But the Furies will have none of it, storm out at these upstart gods who have broken ancient laws, and vent their rage by casting a

curse on the entire land. Aeschylus neatly leaves us with the problem
of determining how these Furies shall be domesticated into human
life so that, honored instead of despised, they may become the
friends and not the enemies of mankind.[17]

In working with this story, and with another story concerning
Oedipus who unwittingly slew his father and married his mother,
thus incurring a similar curse,[18] the three great tragedists reflect a
change that was coming over Greek thought.

Aeschylus, about 525 to 456 B. C., is the oldest of the three. The
primitive conceptions of Homer and Hesiod had failed to satisfy
the more thoughtful men of Aeschylus' time. His problem is to
reconcile the popular religion and the more advanced conceptions
of his day. To that end he portrays Zeus as sublime, all-powerful,
embodying the universal law of justice. No man can escape that law.
Guilt is hereditary. When once the guilt has been incurred, a curse
descends along the family line of that man, yet not in such a way
as to override his power of choice. Aeschylus would be rid of the
notion of conflict between the gods of Olympus and those of the
underworld, putting eternal reason and eternal justice on the throne.

Sophocles, the next great tragedist (497-406 B. C.), is less confident. Certainly the world is governed by divine laws, and Zeus
presides. But Sophocles has less optimism than Aeschylus regarding
the fate of the innocent. To Aeschylus punishment is visited upon
one who is responsible for sin, but to Sophocles, suffering can be
unmerited.

Euripides, about 485 to 407 B. C., strikes straight at the system
by which it was believed the will of the gods was made known, that
is, the system of oracles and divination. The gods, exacting such
unreasonable sacrifices of men, and pursuing men so relentlessly,
had become hateful to men. They made known their will to men,
it was held, by oracles. If this was error, then all built upon it was

error. Is Zeus just? Euripides is not sure. But of one thing he is certain: oracles and divination are no way to learn *whether* he is or not.[19]

Then after tragedy, comedy brought its battery to bear upon the question. When was there ever such a "religious" drama as *The Frogs* of Aristophanes! To him, the gods are not good, not evil, but only ludicrous. To him the nether world is not torture, not bliss, only comic. Athenians, long skeptical of the old mythology, and disarmed by such men as Euripides, must have roared with laughter as they saw travelers to the next life crossing the river amid horseplay, accompanied by a chorus of croaking frogs, and arriving in a world which the mighty gods had made to have neither reason nor tragedy, but only absurdity.

With such laughter as their farewell, the gods died—those earthborn gods whom the Greeks had made responsible for man's plight. But what laughter it was! As has been said of Mark Twain, so here; this laughter had no sound of joy or clear-eyed humor. It was the raucous noise which men make as they go out into the dark, and who in going can make no sense out of either the light or the dark.

In short, when the Greeks made the gods responsible for man's situation, the point they reached was spelled out in one word: *Nonsense*, to the Greeks more dreadful than tragedy.

THE CONFLICT INTERNALIZED

In ancient religions and philosophies there is another great body of thought which places the ultimate responsibility, not outside of, but within, individual man himself.

This was the case in Greece. As popular religion decayed, and as the gods became discredited, Greek thought, at least in the case of the philosophers, turned from the gods to the direct study of man and nature. The names of Socrates, Plato, and Aristotle stand highest among that little group of immortals who, doing their work in Greece, set the stage for man's estimate of himself and his situation in so many other lands and for so many succeeding centuries.

Few men of thought have so seized the imagination as Socrates. He knew full well that he was a public nuisance, and called himself "the gadfly of Athens" because he so exasperated men with his questions. Again he dubbed himself a midwife to men, for he was helping to bring thought to birth; then afterward he stood by and aided in determining whether the thing born was worthy to live or was a mere "wind egg." In this quest, Socrates was concerned always to slough off the irrelevant or the untrue or the partly true, in order that he might arrive at true knowledge.

We know Socrates chiefly through Plato, his disciple. In the famous dialogues of Plato, Socrates often is the principal speaker, but we cannot know when it is Plato speaking and when it is the authentic Socrates. Hence for our purpose we may sum it all up as being Plato's teaching, though usually he has put into the mouth of Socrates matters relevant to our inquiry.

In order to see how Plato made man responsible for his own destiny, we must consider man as Plato saw him; thus also we can understand what the nature of conflict is, as Plato viewed it.

Plato's man consists of body and soul. The soul is pre-existent, and immortal; but it takes up its dwelling place in a body, and upon leaving one body the soul will make its abode in another body, of man or beast depending upon the soul's virtue in its last body. The highest end the soul can achieve is to know absolute goodness, absolute justice, absolute beauty, and so on; that is, to know the absolute "ideas" of which visible things are but shadows.

The soul has four faculties. The lowest is perception, which is possible by the exercise of the bodily senses, but which can deal only with the shadows of true ideas. The next is faith or conviction, which relates to opinion, not to knowledge. The third is understanding, which works with hypotheses, as in geometry and cognate sciences; that is, with the arts. It yields us images of reality, but not yet the true reality itself. The highest faculty is reason, which can arrive at knowledge of ideas, or true being, by means of dialectic. It reaches the first principles of the whole.[20]

With Plato the body is a drag upon the soul. The soul does not attain truth through the senses, but through reason, the highest faculty. The soul attains to the best knowledge of absolute goodness, and the other absolute ideas, when the ultimate vision is so ordered as to have the most exact conception of the essence of each thing to be considered. Such a man, using reason, is most likely to attain to the knowledge of true being. But while we are in the body and as long as the soul is infested with the evils of the body, the desires of the soul will not be satisfied. Wars and other evils result from the lusts of the body. Purification is the separation and release of the soul from the body. The true philosopher therefore is always occupied with the practice of dying in order that he may abandon the body and enter upon the knowledge of true being.[21]

Thus in Plato the conflict is between soul and body. He develops this conception at length in a famous passage comparing the soul to a pair of winged horses and a charioteer. Apparently the charioteer stands for the mind, or reason, or perhaps for what is now often called the ego. The steeds themselves are mixed, not being of equal character. "One of them is noble and of noble origin, and the other is ignoble and of ignoble origin." Again he says that one of the horses is good, the other bad. The first, well conditioned, is erect and well formed, with a lofty neck, an aquiline nose, is white of color with dark eyes, and loves honesty, modesty, and true temperance. He needs no touch of the whip, but is guided by word and admonition.

Not so the other steed. This horse is a large, misshapen animal, put together in any fashion. His neck is short and strong, his face is flat, his color is dark, his eyes are gray and bloodshot. He is the mate of insolence and pride, is shag-eared and deaf, and hardly yields to blow or spur.

The charioteer has no end of trouble in managing the pair. This is the more so because it is of the nature of the soul to grow wings, in order that the soul may soar aloft, may enter the place of true knowledge, beholding absolute justice, temperance, and knowledge, and may feed upon them. But in the flight of the soul to its true place and destiny, the evil steed, if he has not been perfectly trained by the charioteer, gravitates toward the earth. This is the hour of the soul's agony and extreme conflict. For such a soul, sinking earthward, becomes enmeshed in turmoil. Souls then plunge and tread on one another, each seeking to be first, and many, through the ill driving of the charioteer, are lamed or have their wings broken.

Having failed to behold truth, these souls lose their wings and sink to earth, in forgetfulness and vice. It is ordained that the soul cannot return to the place whence it came in less than ten thousand years, during which she must live under correction and probation, lest a worse fate befall her and she pass into the form of some yet lowlier man, or even a beast.

Meanwhile, in exile, memories of what she has seen and known never completely desert the soul. She passes the time of her exile in homesickness for God and true being, a nostalgia which often she herself scarcely understands; for memory has grown dim, and she sees the heavenly counterparts around her only "through a glass dimly." So the soul passes its long years, imprisoned in the body as in an oyster shell, having so far forgotten as to be mystified by now beholding innocence, calm, and happiness, which seem to her to be but apparitions.[22]

Seldom has so powerful a figure been constructed to set forth the conviction that man himself is the battlefield! For Plato there is conflict between soul and body; within the soul there is conflict between rational and irrational. No longer is it Apollo and Dionysus struggling for a man in the heavens above him. Powers no different in nature, but with a different name, struggle in the soul itself. And Plato knows of a release, but it is to be had only at the price of fleeing the body.

This Platonic conception, with its many modifications and outgrowths, was to exert an extraordinary influence upon later Christian thought, coming in, oddly enough, under the pseudonym of another Dionysius who took that name not from the Greek god but from a character whom Paul encountered at Athens, this later "pseudo-Dionysius" standing for the complete opposite of all that the Greek god Dionysus was, standing instead for a revised Platonic doctrine of flight from the body into the Absolute. But that is another story.

Here two chief points in Plato's doctrine are to be observed. For one thing, the nature of man being what it is, man himself and not any outside power is responsible for man's own destiny. But, as a second great proposition, in order to achieve his highest and only true end man must work out his destiny through rationality, must deny the place of the irrational in nature, must deny the worth of the body and seek release of soul from body. Life, as the best man envisions it, is possible only by release from life as common men knew it. So Plato nipped a budding growth in human history, *i. e.,* the study of man as an irrational being.

Aristotle, of course, diverges from Plato in regard to the environing world; Plato would flee it, Aristotle would know it. Further, he was more tolerant of men's passions than Plato. But one basic proposition which chiefly concerns us here he holds in common with

Plato, namely, that man himself is responsible for his own situation. Soul does not mean the same for the two men. For Aristotle the soul has no pre-existence, and has no existence apart from the body, yet it is not one with the body. The relation between soul and body is expressed by the term "entelechy," meaning absoluteness, perfect realization, actual realization as contrasted with potentiality. This may be compared with modern conceptions such as "perfect functioning," or the "life principle." Indeed, much that is put forward in recent times has its roots in, or at least a kinship with, Aristotle: as with Bergson's *elan vital,* and McDougall's "hormic psychology" with its stress upon striving and goal seeking.

The highest end of man, with Aristotle, is happiness; and happiness is activity of the soul in keeping with virtue. Virtue is of two kinds, since the soul is partly rational and partly irrational. Moral virtue has to do with irrational desires which may be made obedient to reason, by prudence. The other virtue, intellectual, is guided by wisdom. So reason keeps its supremacy, as with Plato. But at least the irrational has been accepted, not denied. It has been domesticated, so to speak, somewhat as Aeschylus had tried to do with the Furies in his drama *Eumenides.* And happiness, be it repeated, is activity, guided to be sure both by prudence and by wisdom, but not to be attained by a complete flight from irrationality.[23]

Thus Aristotle, although he agrees with Plato in regarding man as responsible, does not reach the same pessimism concerning human life as Plato, since the former can accept an irrational element in human nature.

Through Thomas Aquinas, Aristotle's teaching also flowed into Christianity, as did Plato's through Plotinus and pseudo-Dionysius. But great as was Aristotle's influence upon thinkers, it was his fate even then to be but dimly understood, and he seems never to have taken hold upon ordinary Christians as Plato did. For as the poet

Gray once remarked, reading Aristotle is like reading a table of contents; it tastes for all the world like chopped hay. Plato at least could be understood by troubled folk in that part of his teaching which counseled that the soul, finding the body to be no true friend, had best fly away from it to heaven and immortality.

So, in later times, many a Christian disturbed by his own volcanic emotions was drawn to a Platonic and ascetic view of life, left family and work-a-day responsibilities in order to seek liberation of the soul by mortification of the body. And many such were to discover then that denying the irrational, so placid-seeming on the philosopher's pages, was in reality a thing of hell and torture.

There were still other ancient bodies of thought in the Graeco-Roman world which took up a position concerning the nature of conflict and the ultimate responsibility for it. One such was Stoicism. Conflict, as the Stoic saw it, was between reason and emotion. In that sense the Stoic admitted the irrational into human nature. He proposed to conquer emotion by minimizing its importance. Emotions were not a part of life in its finally significant aspect; they were rather like stage-play, vivid enough for a moment, but soon gone. It was not emotions that left traces on the tablets of time.

Individual man himself, and man alone, was responsible for the outcome of his own conflict. No outside power could make him good or bad. As Marcus Aurelius often put it, a man's part was to act in keeping with his nature, his spirit. But what is "nature"? The word had a rather technical meaning for the Stoic. It caught up much that was implied in the ancient conception of Fate, as well as much else which modern man intends to convey by the term "evolution," or "principle of growth." Nature meant God to the Stoic, and meant All in a pantheistic sense.

Thereby the Stoic made his own peculiar dilemma. He obligated himself to act in keeping with nature, or the All; yet in that All the irrational as well as the rational was retained! By setting himself to live out only that which he considered rational, and to live down what he viewed as irrational, he re-enacted within himself the conflict which he had quietly admitted into God's own character. Thus he had, as it were, an upper part of God in conflict with a lower part of God.[24]

On such a basis the problem of conflict finally is insoluble. The best that one can do is to defy the lower part of God by being a sort of combined gentleman and hero. This is not to deny the appeal which Stoicism makes even now to many men of noble thought. Still less does it deny the nobility of character in many of its ancient adherents, who deemed life irrational but who took it without whimpering. Now, as then, the chin of the Stoic is up, ready to receive whatever blows nature may deliver. But also, now as then, the Stoic is left to wonder whether in fact there truly is a Friend either within or behind the phenomena of nature.[25]

It remains to speak of one other ancient religion, living still, which addresses itself to the question we are here examining; that is, Buddhism. Brahmanism, the parent religion, had become legalistic, cluttered with an apparatus of sacrificial and other ritual. Both Jainism and Buddhism were revolts which represent the seeking of an internal solution for a conflict which is recognized as being within individual man.

Gautama, after his enlightenment called "the Buddha," taught his "four great truths." The first has to do with the nature of sorrow. All the crucial events and times of human existence are sorrow, he seems to be saying; for death is sorrow, but so is birth, so is sickness, and so is clinging to earthly things. Second, birth and rebirth are the result of the thirst for life, passion, and desire. Third, the only way of escape from the thirst is by the annihilation of desire. Fourth, and more specifically, the way of escape lies along the Eightfold

Path, which consists of ethical teaching: right belief, right resolve, right word, right act, right life, right effort, right thinking, and right meditation.

Thus is attained Nirvana, a state whose character is variously explained. Gautama himself would say no more than that it is the extinction of lust, anger, and ignorance. But he left the way open for those of his followers who so chose, to teach that it means complete extinction, absolute annihilation. Consistent with his own teaching, Gautama held that the great awakening is to become a pessimist.[26]

This is to say that in Buddhism not only is the conflict within the individual, but the conflict itself is evil, and the only complete release consists of annihilation of the being who suffers the conflict, whether that annihilation be regarded as absorption of the soul into the All with consequent loss of individuality, or be regarded as absolute extinction.

Thus among those we have considered, who view the basic conflict as being within individual man, Buddhism reaches the most radical pessimism of all. Both Jainism and Buddhism in its classic form insist that there are no external gods, and that salvation is within. But there is no release except by destruction of the self. Therefore destruction is the greatest boon which the universe can grant, and is to be sought as the highest good.

THE ANCIENT DILEMMA

We have brought out of the ancient "clinic" a body of records, and now we are to summarize the findings. When man's question had to do with the nature of the conflict by which he was affected, the answers have been varied. But predominantly the conflict was understood in terms of light against darkness, or soul against body, or reason against irrationality.

When the question has had to do with ultimate responsibility for the outcome of the conflict, the two classic answers were that it is outside man, or within man himself.

If the conflict is outside man, the favored view in antiquity was that God or the gods are responsible. Such conflict might be between good spirits and evil spirits, or between the gods when there were many gods, or within the God Himself when there is one Supreme Being. On that road, we saw, man's duty becomes that of appeasing the gods or the evil spirits to divert their wrath, and then of bearing as nobly as he can such blows of Fate as it is in his portion to receive. But we saw as well that in such a view the gods become hateful to men, and the universe at last is Nonsense.

If the conflict is ultimately inside man himself and man is responsible for its outcome, the classic views which we have examined have one common answer: flight. It may be the flight of the soul from the body as with Plato, or the flight into reason as with Aristotle and the Stoics, or flight into destruction as with the Buddhists.

The dilemma of antiquity in its stark form was this: if the gods are responsible, the world is Nonsense. A plague then upon their whole house! A jury of Athenian burghers could render a juster verdict than these loathsome deities. Let the average citizen of the universe have a hand in his own Fate. What then? The alternative, once thought through to its end, gives startling results. If man is responsible, he must flee from himself to find rest. He may become a disembodied soul, or a passionless creature of reason all compounded, or become extinguished altogether.

So in antiquity. What of modern psychological thought upon the problem of the nature of conflict and the seat of responsibility for the outcome?

INDIVIDUAL AND ENVIRONMENT

IN MODERN TIMES, as in ancient, men are divided as to the nature of conflict and the seat of responsibility for its outcome. If space permitted it would be illuminating to observe how far this cleavage of opinion has penetrated into modern life, and what some of the results are.

Since that larger inquiry is not possible here, we restrict ourselves to the field of modern psychology. Whatever the precise definition given to the term, "psychology" occupies itself in some manner, sooner or later, with human beings. What it has to say regarding conflict and responsibility has a direct bearing on questions of guilt, and ultimately on those concerning redemption.

MODERN PSYCHOLOGY

Modern psychology may be regarded as beginning with Descartes in the first half of the seventeenth century. Until well within the nineteenth century it was not a separate branch, but continued to be, generally speaking, a part of philosophy.

Modern psychology inherited the core of its problem from the late Middle Ages. During the Middle Ages, when the Roman Church dominated Europe spiritually and politically, the struggle between reason and authority had disturbed Christians century after century. Even before the church's power was shattered it had become apparent that ecclesiastical authority as an external control of man's life was doomed. The movements known as the Renaissance and Reformation each in its own way had, it was supposed, released man from external authority and set him free to be guided by reason.

But what is this "reason" which was admitted to sovereignty in the modern world in place of the medieval church's authority? What are its capacities and what its limits? The problem of the nature of reason had to be worked out in every respect—politically, socially, religiously, philosophically, and psychologically.

A favorite setting for this question is the further but kindred problem of the relation between mind and body. During the seventeenth century two ancient streams of thought began to emerge in new forms, and with fresh poignancy. One represents the effort to preserve the reality and autonomy of soul, or mind. It is an attempt to guarantee the integrity of the inner world where reason functions. A second stream represents the effort to preserve the reality and importance of physical being and physical processes, such as body, matter, natural laws, and the like. It is an attempt to guarantee the integrity of the objective world of body and environment.

From Descartes to Kant, for about a century and a half previous to 1800, the first of these streams slowly dwindled in importance. Those who sought to guarantee the reality and autonomy of man's inner world tended to be men who approached the problem through the use of logic; and on the whole the results were not impressive. By the time of Berkeley and Hume the proposals being put forward in philosophy had reached the point of absurdity.

If reason could arrive at such strange conclusions, it was time to take fresh stock of reason itself. It was Kant's role to do exactly that. He subjected reason to analyses so penetrating as to leave their mark on all later western thought. And yet Kant's very achievement left reason in a hardly less precarious position than it occupied before. Observe how this was so.

Kant held that knowledge is possible independently of the senses, for the structure of mind is such that we can have knowledge in certain respects prior to experience. Mind is not merely passive in its environment; it is active, transforming the multiplicity of external impressions into ordered thought. But there the difficulty arises. Just *because* it transforms the impressions, the mind can not know "the thing in itself." As Kant put it, "What may be the nature of subjects considered as things in themselves and without reference to the receptivity of our sensibility is quite unknown to us. We know nothing more than our mode of perceiving them."[1] Mind can be absolutely certain of itself, but it can be only "practically" certain of the environment.

This was a severely chastened conception of mind, from the very man who had set out to be its champion. Kant's position seemed an anchor to those who would contend for the reality and power of the inner, mental world. Yet it could be replied at once, "Power or capacity for what? If not capacity to know the outer world with certainty, this is not reason's sovereignty, but reason's abdication." His results, on the one hand, spell certainty, but on the other hand they also spell skepticism, concerning reason.

After Kant had left the capacity of reason in this dubious position, philosophers continued to dispute his meaning and to "reconstruct" his teaching for another hundred years. Thus from Descartes to Kant the very men who had most resolutely set themselves to establish the position of soul, or mind, or inner world, had either fought a losing battle, or at the best interpretation of their results had merely got a negotiated peace. Nor had they left an altogether imposing legacy to their successors.

Meanwhile, as the position of the inner world grew more precarious the outer world began to take over the domination of modern life and thought. The age of science was opening. Practical men, pulses quickened by the newly discovered marvels of the natural world, poured themselves with an increasing tide of energy into their investigations. With this growing impulse went a hearty contempt for the philosopher's uncertainty as to what the scientist could know. He simply acquired his "knowledge," reported it, and went his way amid increasing popular esteem.

It is peculiarly difficult for us who live in this current which is still flowing powerfully, to evaluate it. We ourselves are part of it. We have been influenced by it, and most of us owe physical life, or limb, or at least our bodily comforts, to the results achieved by means of "the scientific approach" in man's mastery of nature. It is in the air we breathe to revere the patient objectivity of the worker who seeks to rule out the personal equation so that he may report his findings in irreproachable tables, graphs, and mathematical formulas. In such an atmosphere it is not easy to reach objectivity concerning our own objectivity; it is far easier to fall down and worship "scientific method," or at the opposite pole to court a cheap notoriety by defaming it.

The history of psychology from about the time of Kant is therefore peculiarly enlightening,[2] for that history suggests what it has cost man, in terms of his own estimate of himself, to study human nature objectively, from without.

The nineteenth century witnessed a trend which had the double results of making psychology an empirical and experimental science with man as object, and of vastly increasing the importance attached to the environment in which man as an object exists. As for the latter—the place given the environment—Darwin's work in accumulating factual data became the envy of all scientists; and his theory concerning the origin of species led men to think in terms of environment and adaptation to environment as never before. As for the former—man as an object in his environment—it came about that many of the leaders in psychology brought to the study a background of work as physiologists, anatomists, or physicists. Thus trained, Johannes Mueller, Ernst H. Weber, von Helmholtz, and Fechner gave great impetus to the experimental study of psychological problems. Wundt established at Leipzig the first laboratory devoted specifically to psychology. He himself lived until the twentieth century, profoundly influencing his students and setting the pace for other universities to follow in the establishment of psychological laboratories. It became the generally, though not universally, accepted dictum that the proper method of psychology is experiment, or measurement, to the end that the results may be stated as quantities.

ACADEMIC PSYCHOLOGY

Within the twentieth century we may distinguish two general lines of development in psychology. One we may call academic psychology, referring thus to the psychology taught in the universities, and providing the theory of human nature for the public school system. For the most part the academic psychology of the twentieth century has taken for granted the premises bequeathed it by the nineteenth century, namely, that man is an object in his environment, to be studied experimentally and quantitatively. The importance of the assumption is illustrated by the syllogism of a university teacher of psychology who has left a deep impress on educational psychology; he was wont to say, "Whatever exists, exists in quantity; whatever exists in quantity can be measured."

Several schools of academic psychology have been influential in this century. One school known as structuralists held that the proper field of study in psychology is consciousness, with its various elements; but these states and elements of consciousness proved hard to manage in objective and quantitative terms, and the school died out.

Three other schools, more or less in rivalry, came to the fore. Each of the three is biologically-minded, has derived much of its information from experiments with animals, and finds it convenient to refer to "the animal," or "the organism," when stating its propositions. One of these schools is that of the functionalists, who are especially interested in the capacity of the animal to adapt itself to the environment. "Mind" has with some consistency dropped out of the vocabulary, and "intelligence" is preferred, a term frequently used to designate the capacity of the animal to make this adaptation to the environment.

Another school, the behaviorist, considers behavior as the proper study of psychology, and in its strict form denies the existence of consciousness. This school occupies itself with the study of stimulus and response, denies general habits such as honesty and the like, and holds that each habit we wish to form must be specifically taught.

A third modern school, called Gestalt psychology, is not yet a complete system, for it has many gaps; but its advocates explain psychological phenomena as far as possible by the laws of physics, and regard the individual as formed by the group, thus heavily weighting the influence of the environment in which, as it were, an individual is shaped and carried along by physically-determined laws.

Although we have called this general line of development by the name of "academic" psychology, we do not imply that it is remote from modern life. On the contrary these three last-named psychologies, singly or combined into some eclectic system, constitute a large part of the teaching presented in colleges to youth as an explanation of their own nature; and they provide a theoretical basis for philosophies of education which in turn underlie much public education.

If now we recall the story of ancient thought as expressed in religions and philosophies, some of our own modern answers to the same questions may take on added significance. It was pointed out that in one major current of thought during ancient times, the responsibility for man's situation was placed out beyond man himself; while in another, the responsibility was seen as being within man himself. Some comparisons, accordingly, may be useful as we seek to orient ourselves not alone in our own time, but in the longer sweep of human thought as well.

Modern academic psychology, as far as we have sketched it here, has exhibited increasingly that ancient and never-ceasing readiness of man by which he is able to interpret his own situation or plight as something imposed upon him from without by means of external forces impinging upon him, relieving him of responsibility and moving him to action independently of his own choosing. Ancient man most readily put his responsibility on the gods. The modern academic psychologist cannot think in that category, but he uses other names for the powers that dominate the individual from without. Man is not obedient to his fate, but is adapting to his environment. Man does not act in response to a god, but in response to a stimulus. The law which he serves and which he seeks to understand is not that of a god, but that of "nature."

Again, modern man as academic psychologist, having disavowed the sovereignty of the inner world, has next performed an act of surprising humility, comparable perhaps to ancient man's obeisance to Fate. For with all solemnity and speaking ex cathedra from the chair of science, this psychologist pronounces that man is an animal, and thence sets forth to explain man to himself by means of experiments with hungry cats in cages striking out with random movements until they hit upon some releasing latch; or experiments with frenzied rats running senseless mazes until by chance they come to food or escape. It was once the fashion to sing in religion's name that we are worms of the dust. To celebrate that view of man's nature in song now brings only disgusted protest. Our lowly estate is illumined, instead, by drawing "laws of learning" from the movements of bewildered animals entrapped by the environment. The Greek, who made the gods responsible for man's plight, finally reached Nonsense as his result. Perhaps the placing of responsibility in the environment, and the conception of man as animal-in-cage-adapting-to-environment, yield us the modern equivalent.

Academic psychology offers no serious interpretation of conflict in the individual. It is true that this psychologist, in his list of instincts, will usually show one or more pairs of instincts which tend in competing directions. But he must go to the environment for an explanation of the activity of one of these instincts and the quiescence of the other. He can give no good account of "will," for he fears it is but another name for a "faculty" of mind, and all faculties of mind are taboo. He can understand that there are conflicts in the environment, and he likes to measure the strength and interplay of these conflicts outside of the individual. But if he reckons at all with conflict in the individual it is likely to be in terms of external inducements. Although in one breath he disavows mind, in the next breath he will urge that reason's true sway as exemplified in scientific method will heal these conflicts in the environment, and hence, of course, bring peace to the individual who is a sort of condensed replica of the social whole. But for any penetrating light upon the divided self we must seek elsewhere.

Hence it has come about in modern times that academic psychology offers the surest way one can find for a man to avoid any radical understanding of himself or of his fellows. It permits him in the name of science to lose himself in his environment, becoming submerged in statistical studies of man as a responding animal. This branch of psychology represents the virtually complete triumph of the outer world, and the equally complete self-abnegation of those who deny that the inner world has any sovereignty even over itself.

This is the more meaningful because it appears to give scientific sanction to that philosophy which elevates the all-powerful State to the position of God. A fountainhead of this doctrine in its modern form was Hegel in Germany. Hegel's teaching started upon a wooing note, calculated to win the ear of enlightened men. His thesis was that reason governs and always has governed the world. God Himself is reason, eternal Wisdom. What is intended by reason is accomplished in two domains: that of nature, and that of spirit. Accordingly, reason cannot be understood apart from spirit. The essence of spirit is freedom; spirit has its center in itself; it has no unity outside itself. Spirit is self-contained existence, and exactly this is freedom. I am free only when my existence depends on myself. This self-contained existence is none other than self-consciousness. Universal history is "the exhibition of spirit in the process of working out the knowledge of that which it is potentially."

With Hegel the material in which the idea of freedom is wrought out is personality, *i. e.,* the subjective will. The subjective will can gratify itself only in the moral whole, the State. The State is "that form of reality in which the individual has and enjoys his freedom, but on the condition of his recognizing, believing in, and willing that which is common to the whole." The State is the divine Idea as it exists on earth, says Hegel; and only the individual who obeys the law of the State is truly free. True freedom allows no reflection by the individual—only obedience to the State.[3]

From his respected chair of philosophy at Berlin so did Hegel teach, and tilled the soil well for the springing up of the totalitarian

State. It became an act of reverence to believe that the only freedom possible to man depended upon his conformity to that environing, commanding State. And as we have already implied, academic psychology, professing to speak in the name of Science, brought its laurels too and helped to crown the Environment as Lord of All. "Professing themselves to be wise, they became fools."

Depth Psychology

But all was not well with the "free" personality who was citizen of the modern State in the nineteenth and twentieth centuries. The dehumanized society, the revolutionized industry, and the Leviathan State which he was creating were rapidly making his environment into a monster that now began to terrify its human creator.

The dim forebodings that arose in the early part of the nineteenth century are symbolized in a novel by Mary Godwin Shelley, published in 1818. Frankenstein, a young student of physiology, undertook to create life by artificial means. He took corpses from the church graveyard and the dissecting room, formed a body out of the materials, and endowed it with soulless animal life by galvanism. This creature was frantic with unsatisfied human longings, became a monster, turned upon its creator, pursued him from land to land, and at last wrought a dreadful vengeance upon the one who had made him.

So the modern environment began to exact its toll from the men who had first created it, then deified it, but who had left themselves no soul with which to defy it. The plight of those suffering from various forms of nervous and mental illness commenced to attract attention, and to raise the question of cause and cure. Whether these illnesses are more frequent in our time than in previous centuries is a query that must remain unanswered. But certainly the situation of these persons was forced upon the public view as not before, especially by Pinel in France and by Dorothea Lynde Dix in America.[4]

From influences such as these and many others, a second general line of development began to emerge late in the nineteenth century, and has spread widely in the twentieth century. It has had various names such as the new psychology, medical psychology, clinical psychology, depth psychology, and so on. No one term is entirely satisfactory, as the movement has numerous branches, each regarding itself as the only true light and giving its own name to one particular type of thought and practice. It has been especially influenced by Pierre Janet, Sigmund Freud, Carl G. Jung, Alfred Adler, and Otto Rank. Some of the differences between the respective schools founded by these men are very significant for our line of inquiry concerning guilt and redemption, as will be pointed out in due course.

But in reference to the movement as a whole we shall use the term "depth psychology" to serve as a reminder that a "new" psychology has arisen out of clinical experience at the very time when man's thinking concerning himself was leaving him no soul, while the environment which he was making and deifying was conspiring to crush this entrapped animal.

This depth psychology takes its point of departure, not from the environment, but from the plight of actual persons who are ill. It has shown itself ready, perhaps much too ready, to go far beyond this basis and generalize for all persons and all times. But at least its field of primary concern is man's inner world of experience as contrasted with the environing world of objective reality.

It appears to be due chiefly to depth psychology that the concept of *relationship* has come to hold a place of such crucial importance in psychiatry, social work, education, and criminology, in so far as these fields have felt the influence of this psychology. The individual is seen as always existing in relation to other individuals. An almost endless range of relationships exists between the individual and the other persons and groups with whom he has association; and none of these relationships is excluded from consideration. But in clinical experience certain relationships are found to be especially dynamic and determinative; particularly such as son to mother, son to father, daughter to mother, daughter to father; mother to son, father to son, mother to daughter, father to daughter; husband to wife, wife to husband; and the relationships between siblings, that is, children of the same parents, such as oldest child to second child, second child to oldest child, and so on.

These dynamic relationships are characterized by intense emotion; and it is found in clinical experience that the emotion is "ambivalent," that is, containing both love and hate, affection and hostility. Depth psychology attaches great importance to feelings and emotions. No possible shade of feeling or intensity of emotion is neglected, but the various schools differ in the particular types and sources of emotion to which they devote principal attention.

The Freudian has been remarkably fascinated by the discovery that human beings have organs of sex and excretion, and emotions connected therewith. Orthodox disciples of Freud never weary of the subject, having created for it a body of theory and a vocabulary which are like nothing else ever brought forth on earth.

But the movement is breaking away from the Freudian obsession with these organs and their functions, and seeks to reckon with every emotion of which the human being is capable. From clinical experience this psychology can be said to have demonstrated that man does not thrive at all except as he thrives emotionally.

Furthermore, emotions and "the unconscious" are viewed as closely associated, and depth psychology lays great emphasis on the unconscious. Doctrines of the unconscious had already been elaborated in philosophy before the twentieth century, partly in protest against the view that reason is supreme. Leibniz, Schopenhauer, and von Hartmann had contributed to this trend in philosophy before it was brought into psychology by F. W. H. Myers and developed by Freud and Jung. It is insisted that we are ruled by our unconscious far more than by our conscious mind; that we cover our motives over with a thick coating of "reasons," and that the products of reason are of doubtful value. It is contended that we express our own true selves and motives, not so much through our reasoning in words, as through symbols such as those of dreams, art, poetry, music, gestures, wit, and the like.

The nature of the unconscious is variously conceived. With Schopenhauer it is the will to live, and finally the will to sleep in the will-less peace of death; the unconscious is malignant, driving men to suffering.[5] In depth psychology, especially in Jung, the unconscious is thought of as benevolent, our own true nature seeking to express itself. With Jung the racial unconscious looms large; it attempts to direct us toward a manner of living in which we can find wholeness; thus the racial unconscious seems to equate with God. Elsewhere generally in this movement the unconscious is held to be neither moral nor immoral in itself, but is essentially a striving for ends that will yield preservation and health.

Conflict is recognized by this psychology as being the common lot of man. The nature of the most basic conflict is variously explained. Some of the more important differences may be seen if we distinguish between the sources of conflict and the structure of the self in which the conflict occurs.

Speaking in the broadest terms, depth psychology sees three chief sources of conflict. One is the primitive impulses, which have been so greatly stressed by the Freudians. Except for the Freudians, the proposition that sex lies at the basis of *all* conflict is now commonly regarded as disproved. This certainly does not minimize the significance of such conflicts as unmistakably root in this source, but it does away with the one-sided view that all conflict has its origin in this part of man's nature.

Another great source of human conflict may be summarized as the desire for emotional security, particularly in the most dynamic relationships such as son to mother, and so forth. The forms of this conflict are myriad, and to sum them up in any one phrase is likely to hide their intricacy. Conflict may arise in infancy, as when one does not feel himself safe in the affection of mother or father. It may be fanned in any later years of life whenever one does not win his coveted recognition and esteem, whatever the guerdon he desires may be. But it must be repeated that summary statements such as these have only a limited value; for the complicated nature of actual emotional conflict is only to be seen in the living human being himself. Even the clinical record of it is only a pale shadow at best. In later lectures we shall get a closer view of these conflicts with their intricate patterns and their destructive emotions.

Still another source of conflict is competing emotions existing within the same individual and directed toward one and the same object. That object may be the individual himself or other individuals. Thus some, as Freud and his followers, see one's own basic emotions toward himself as being in conflict; they have come to speak of a life instinct and a death instinct; and they hold that originally these conflicting instincts, or the emotions of love and hate, are turned inward upon the self, but may become diverted outward toward other objects.

Others see conflicting emotions in the most dynamic relationships which one person sustains to others. Rank, for example, attached great significance to the conflict between two kinds of love. One is Eros, the love which demands and absorbs, using others for one's own ends and thus containing an element of disguised *self* love; it results in the warping or dwarfing both of the one thus loving, and the other persons whom one loves in this manner. The other kind of love is Agape, love which is outgoing, self-giving, desiring most of all the well-being of the loved person. It is directed toward another as he is, and by that very fact creates a fundamental sense of worth in the person so loved.[6] These conflicting emotions, whether the life wish and the death wish directed to oneself, or Eros and Agape toward another, are seen as struggling with each other while civilization with its deep irrationalities has unfolded, and as contending now for mastery in the individual.

As for the structure of the self in which the conflict occurs, two positions have been set forth, by Freud and Jung respectively, which have proved influential outside the schools of these particular men.

Toward the end of his life Freud came to think of the self as embracing what he called the id, the ego, and the superego. The term "id" refers to the archaic and elemental impulses emanating from the unconscious. The "superego" represents the dictates of society, but especially those of one's parents. It is the sense of "I ought," containing the specific details of the code one has received from parents and society, and is surrounded with deep emotional sanctions. The "ego," the core of the personal self, must find a way to balance one's personal living between the claims of his own unconscious and those of the superego.

Although he does not use the same terms for it, Jung deals with essentially the same conflict between the demands of the unconscious and those of the environment, but points out that the solution cannot be the same for all individuals. He sees a basic difference between individuals according as one is extraverted or introverted. The extravert is oriented by his environment, directs his interest toward objective happenings and data, and is governed by what others think, feel, say, or do. The introvert is oriented by subjective factors. He is not so much governed by the environment as he is by his own response to it. He trusts his own thinking, his own intuitions, his own feeling.[7] The difference between extravert and introvert is not the same as the difference between unselfish and selfish persons, as it has often been taken to be. The extravert may be either selfish or unselfish, and so with the introvert. Rather, attention is directed to differing centers of gravity in living, according as one gives primacy either to his environment or to his inner, subjective world.

Concerning the nature of conflict, then, it is commonly held in this psychology that conflict exists first of all within man himself, because of man's own inherent nature. Indeed, it has become an axiom in depth psychology that conflict *is* within the individual, and that the effort to push the conflict out beyond oneself, locating it within the environment and regarding oneself as the victim of that environment, is itself a mark of man's sickness. Primarily the plight is an inner one, within man himself. Man, individual man, is often likened to a civil war. As Menninger puts it, the case is that of "man against himself"; or in Jung's phrase, modern man is "in search of a soul."

If the seat of conflict is viewed as being within man himself, where does responsibility for its solution lie? Here depth psychology breaks with the streams of thought which we have thus far examined, and introduces a conception of major significance. It can be stated thus, with two points of emphasis.

First, responsibility for the solution of his conflict lies with the individual himself. It is constantly emphasized that if one does not actively take a hand in the solution of his own conflicts, they will not be solved. A man's conflicts cannot be solved *for* him apart from his own participation. The solution cannot be handed him by means of advice. Growth comes, it is unremittingly urged, as one accepts responsibility for his own situation, for the solution of his own conflicts, and for the outcomes of his own living.

But, second—and this is the chief point of difference between depth psychology and the other lines of thought concerning responsibility which we have examined—*this responsibility must be borne in a relationship* with one or more other individuals. What the second individual in this relationship must do, or what he must be, is not a matter of general agreement in depth psychology, and some of the most important meanings that lie behind our general statement must be reserved for consideration later and in other connections. Here it will suffice to state some equally general, but essential, qualifications.

The two points of view in depth psychology which we have just mentioned—that responsibility for the solution of his own conflicts rests with the individual, and that this responsibility must be borne in a relationship with one or more other individuals—separates this position from others which may seem to resemble it. Depth psychology regards a particular person as an individual, but not as a solitary unit who can be treated as if he existed altogether apart from his environment. It holds that the environment must supply at least one other person to enter into the healing relationship with the ill person, but it does not naïvely suppose that manipulating the environment will solve the individual's conflicts.

We have already said that depth psychology has built its position largely out of the cases of persons who are sick in some respect in their emotions. Now we must add that therapists tend to believe that the service of a person especially trained to enter the healing relationship with an ill individual is required in modern society chiefly *because* some other dynamic relationships which the individual has already sustained were unwholesome in their emotional character. We say "chiefly," since hereditary constitutional factors must always be reckoned with. But it seems that the principal causes underlying nervous and mental diseases are, with increasing unanimity, attributed to malignant emotions in human relationships. Indeed, the range of illnesses once thought of as "purely physical" in character but now laid at the door of emotional stresses, appears to be increasing. And by the same token therapists tend to believe that if the most intimate and dynamic relationships of the individual are emotionally wholesome, his general emotional and physical health is rendered probable, almost to the point of assurance.

Depth psychology thus attributes crucial importance not only to the dynamic relationships which an individual sustains, particularly in his very early life; but also believes that it is the emotional character of those relationships which *makes* them dynamic, with power either to build life up or to thwart it. And in proportion as one is ill in his emotions, he has need of another person, especially trained for the part, who will enter a healing relationship with that individual.[8]

THE PERSPECTIVE

We have now surveyed, after a fashion, a small part of the vast sweep of human thought from ancient to modern times concerning two questions which man seems unable to cease asking, whether that man be the ancient Oriental working at these issues in terms of mythology, or the modern Occidental attacking them with the tools of scientific method. These two questions as we have put them, to say it again, are, what is the nature of the conflict in which man finds himself, and where does responsibility for its solution lie? We have already summarized some of the views held in antiquity.

In this lecture we have dealt, as space permitted, with the views of modern psychologists, they being men who have set themselves professionally to work with human nature. We have seen that as in ancient times, so now even when using scientific method instead of myths and philosophies, men still are not able to agree either as to the nature of man's most basic conflict, or as to the responsibility for its existence and its solution.

Oddly enough, those psychologists who have most vigorously insisted that their work is scientific get results strikingly similar to views held by Greeks and others in past millenniums, who put the conflict outside of man himself and then could find no way to solve it, arriving finally at Nonsense. For in the last analysis it does not make a great difference whether the Nonsense is conceived as due to our being men at the mercy of a pack of stupid gods, or as due to our being animals bereft of rationality, trapped by a social environment gone mad, and terrorized by a physical environment of tremendous power in the hands of a crazy society. If man has thought to absolve himself of responsibility for his own plight and thus to dignify himself in his own eyes, we may fairly ask whether he has accomplished more toward that end when he acted as academic psychologist in modern times, than he did in previous ages by means of myth.

Depth psychology, on the other hand, convinced that the basic conflicts of human existence are in individual man himself, seeing these conflicts as first of all emotional in nature, and regarding man as responsible for the solution of his own conflicts, is optimistic as far as it maintains that conflicts of the most basic character are capable of being resolved in a suitable relationship if they can be got at in time. It is confident, too, that this view is well supported by clinical experience.

And yet it is notable that some of the most pessimistic outlooks encountered in modern times are to be found among these same persons, especially as expressed in their writings. Since they have such ground for optimism, the reasons for so deep a pessimism must be sought.

Those reasons, it appears, lie along two kindred lines. One has to do with the nature of the society in which the dynamic relationships between individuals exist. Society develops from more simple to more complex. But as society grows more complex it seems to lose whatever capacity it had, in its simpler forms, for healing the damage which its own ongoing life produces. In a more complex society the damage done by a malignant relationship outruns the capacity of that same society to repair the ravages wrought by that malignant relationship.

Thus far depth psychology has not demonstrated that it conceives how society can supply its own deficiency in this respect. Individual workers, in many instances, have far-reaching insights, but these insights have only begun to find expression in publication, and it seems fair to say that the published material still is heavily weighted with pessimism concerning society, in so far as society receives attention at all. These writings tend to give one the impression that depth psychology understands society as a thwarter well enough—thwarting man's sexual impulses and thwarting his desire for emotional security. Depth psychology is familiar enough with, and has good insight into, a society which is running down of exhaustion and destroying itself by its own malignant relationships. But thus far it seems feeble in its groping for any way by which the process of social self-destruction might be reversed.

Freud, for example, is not the only pessimist among these people, but his pessimism is profound. Freud sees society's code as stimulating conflict in the individual which would not exist if man could only "be himself." But for the individual man to "be himself" in the Freudian sense seems to mean remaining unmatured, and therefore to lead not to social well-being but to social chaos, as Ibsen showed in his play *Peer Gynt*. To Freud, though, society is evil because of what it does to persons; but Freudian man, the unmatured man, by being himself seeks primarily for his own well-being, and for that reason could never create a society profoundly different from the one we now know. Freud's pessimism therefore is more radical even than that of the Buddhist. The Buddhist at least can respectably seek to flee from desire and achieve his own annihilation. But to Freud no evil could be greater than to flee from the reality of desire, yet desire as the ruling motive can create no world where desire may be satisfied except as the animal might sate itself and then lie down to rest.[9]

Here we reach the second ground of pessimism in depth psychology, namely, the fact that by its own premises it has so largely deflated or even disavowed reason. We have said that many writers in this psychology seem to know no society which is capable of repairing its own damage as it grows older and more complex. This is so partly because of what has been done with reason in making up the picture of the human individual. If one may trust impressions and overtones rather than depending upon specific utterances, it would often seem that feeling has been admitted to sovereignty in place of reason, and that the individual is expected to be his own legislator, executive, and judiciary in the government of himself. But if this is done, and in the extent to which the individual is expected to take such a role, there appears to be no bridge by which to arrive at a "rational" society without harmfully curtailing the freedom which the individual's welfare demands. Then, in turn, we have the problem known in modern parlance as "pure individualism," with all rights guaranteed to the individual and none guaranteed to society. The result finally is a society in which individuals perish. This, it may be, is one of the prices paid for the conviction that man's proper destiny is to flee from reason.

But if there is ground for radical pessimism in much psychological thought concerning man and society, it is to be borne in mind that there is also one ground for true optimism in that same body of thought, as we have already shown. For the assurance comes from the clinic that *man's conflicts are capable of being resolved within a suitable relationship.* As far as the present survey of thought is concerned, we encountered this conception first in depth psychology. But in the whole of human experience it was not *first* met in that setting, nor has all been said of it there that is to be said. It will confront us again.

Taking it as a whole, however, it is a strange story which has unfolded since the Renaissance—this story of modern man's attempt to understand himself. It is the story of a search, a conquest, and then of a bewilderment such as has seldom come upon mankind. That story, already hastily told and now hastily re-sketched for emphasis, is this:

Passionately seeking freedom, man declared the autonomy of the individual, who was thenceforth to rule himself and his world by reason. Then he fled reason, reporting himself to be a creature ruled by his emotions. He broke the external authority of a totalitarian church, and then set up in its stead the crushing authority of the totalitarian state, a desperate effort to fill the vacuum created in human society by the human effort to find fulfillment through Eros love alone. The thing he has created—his own social environment of which he is part, and society's use of nature's resources as a means for social suicide—this thing terrifies him, as a ghastly nightmare does. But he can come to no clear verdict as to his own responsibility for all that has overtaken him.

This story of modern man's attempt to understand himself is one in which psychology is only a part, but truly a part. Accordingly, let the psychologist now be thought of as man speaking forth concerning himself, after a prolonged attempt to comprehend himself in his modern setting. In this role, as psychologist, man has passed verdict upon himself, finding that he has deep kinship with the animal creation, but beyond that, dubious of his own capacity and divided within himself as to the responsibility which attaches to his own acts and feelings. Let this psychologist represent modern man as highly educated, acquainted with science and trained in its methods, at home in his world but critical of that world, and seeking a rational grasp of the individual's place in nature and in society. We say "seeking a rational grasp," for it should be obvious that a substantial capacity for reasoning is required in one who disavows that he is a creature of reason.

Then let individual persons, in conflict and struggling with profound feelings of guilt, represent modern man, whether educated or illiterate, striving to solve emotionally and within himself the same problems which the psychiatrist, for example, seeks to help the patient solve. The patient is, literally, the sufferer, suffering from the very thing which the psychologist among others is attempting to understand and heal.

The patient, though, has been overwhelmed by the tides and storms of his own emotions. This sufferer, whether he comes to the psychiatrist or to the minister, may or may not retain all his capacity for clear thinking, but his thinking brings him no relief, for one surge of emotions within him sweeps away such little structures of reason as he had erected. He thinks to settle his strife by acknowledging supreme allegiance to God or state or some other deity, as his case may be, and then acting; only to find himself torn with emotions for and against himself. He had hoped to satisfy Eros, but had only succeeded in establishing another bond of an infantile sort, which he then resents, and yet tries to "drink dry." He acquits himself of all blame, as he believes, putting the responsibility upon God or state or heredity or some other entity, only to discover that he cannot forgive himself. Or he admits his responsibility, only to find he is overwhelmed with condemnation of himself.

✢ III ✢

GUILT AS FACT AND FEELING

CERTAIN DIFFERENCES in meaning lie hidden beneath the general term "guilt." These meanings must be distinguished, otherwise a word with variable content soon brings us into ambiguity of thought and confusion of experience. Guilt may refer to fact, or to responsibility, or to feeling; or to combinations of these.

When the question of fact is involved, "guilt" implies that one has done something forbidden or failed to do something required. The "something" may be action, or it may be feeling. The source of the prohibition or requirement may be religious, or legal, or social, or familial, or personal; and may exist in written form, or as unwritten law.

When the question of responsibility is uppermost, "guilt" indicates that one is held accountable by himself or by others for doing or feeling what was forbidden, or for failing to do or to feel what was required; and it often implies that one is accountable also for consequences that later ensue.

As feeling, "guilt" refers to the emotional aspect of the experience of one who stands in judgment upon himself, and condemns himself or at least acknowledges others' condemnation of himself as deserved. The intensity of the emotion may bear little or no apparent relation to the fact with which it is associated; indeed, the frequent disproportion between fact and feeling constitutes one of the most difficult problems met in connection with guilt.

GUILT AS FACT

A young mother, and her son who was some twenty months old, lived with her parents while the husband was in the army. The boy discovered that when he pulled the cord of a window shade the shade would roll up. He was greatly pleased with the sight and noise of the whirring shade, and the other members of the household were as greatly annoyed. Mornings while the grandfather was dressing, the boy would come into the room, grasp the cord, and send the shade rolling up. Forbidding him did no good, and the grandfather began to spank the boy's hand whenever the latter reached for the cord. The slight punishment broke the practice; but afterward the boy would often go to the window, stretch out his left hand toward the cord, then strike his left hand with his right hand, each time saying, "Shade, Da, Da, no, no."

This child was rehearsing and putting into words his form of a conflict so common and so old that no one knows when it began; the conflict between some inherent desire or impulse, and the parental prohibition of it or its expression.

When we refer to "guilt as fact," we have in mind that in such a conflict, individuals often break the requirements of parents, religion, society, or state, thereby incurring whatever measure of blame attaches to the forbidden act or feeling. This is the most immediately obvious aspect of guilt. In its first connotation, guilt points to some specific infraction or failure. One has broken the code.

There is a class of works with which one needs to have at least a speaking acquaintance if he wishes to know how specific these codes are. We refer to such treatises as *The Golden Bough* by Frazer, *Folkways* by Sumner, *The Science of Society* by Sumner and Keller, *A History of Matrimonial Institutions* by Howard, *Medieval Handbooks of Penance* by McNeill and Gamer, and the far older *Mishnah* of orthodox Judaism.

Two features of these codes stand out: their highly specific nature, and the great variety in them when they are taken as a whole. In their specific character, they give abundant evidence of the minutely detailed regulations by which the conduct of the individual is often governed within a given society.

To illustrate is unsatisfactory when the details themselves fill volumes. It will serve the present purpose if we are reminded that the codes reach into virtually every area of common life, such as the persons one may or may not marry, the conduct and feelings required or prohibited in relation to one's parents or those in positions of higher authority, showing the face, contact with the dead, disposal of refuse, what may and what may not be eaten, use of personal names as allowed and as prohibited, parts of the body that may or may not be seen under exactly specified conditions, and so on endlessly.

But, while the codes are so specific when seen one by one, it is notable that they vary so greatly in reference to a given act. To take human life, for example, is severely punished under some circumstances, but is highly praised under others. Sex practices considered outrageous in one culture may be accepted as a matter of course in another. Here again it would be a limitless task to gather all the instances. But when this wide variety is viewed as a whole it gives ground for the statement frequently made, that no act can be selected which has not somewhere been forbidden and condemned, and somewhere else permitted or even approved.

That consideration, in turn, leads one to recognize that, taking the codes as a whole, they represent requirements imposed upon the individual from without, whether the source be regarded as divine or human. Of course it can very often be shown that a particular requirement has a basis in expediency, being designed for individual or social welfare. But even then it remains true that when a given individual comes into life he is confronted by requirements which he had no part in formulating, and which may thwart the expression of some, or many, native impulses.

These points are often emphasized, and justly so. Yet the facts thus far tell us little except that society has formulated its codes and demands that individuals conform. It still remains to ask why the conflict between impulse and prohibition should so often result in distress which apparently is immeasurably more painful than anything comparable in the lower orders of animal existence.

Take, for instance, the conflict between a rigid code of honor, and the native impulses of desire. It has been said many times that such a code of honor as grew up in the time of chivalry did much to "Christianize" war and lust, and doubtless the point can be well supported. But those who lived in the midst of that code's influence must have recognized that internal conflict was increased by the code itself.

This was worked out in dramatic form in *The Cid* by Pierre Corneille, who portrayed the conflict between honor and love, with some of the resulting complications. The dramatist here shows us that the rigid code of honor has made it impossible for the natural impulses of love to eventuate in marriage, until some accident has intervened. It is as if he had said that the code of honor makes it impossible to love honorably.

What the dramatist presents in oversimplified and schematic form, comes out of actual life which is not simple and not schematic, but where the conflict between code and impulse certainly exists. In explanation, it is contended frequently that the individual has incorporated a particular code within himself as his conscience or "superego," and that this is the reason for conflict and for the suffering which results from the guilt feeling. The internalizing of the code can hardly be doubted, any more than the statement that the code itself is composed of particulars which are not the same for all times and places.

But we still must ask *why* violating the internalized code often brings so painful an aftermath. And the question gains a yet sharper edge when it is remembered that the code itself has not been uniform among all men and in all times. If the codes themselves have not been uniform, and if violating the code is sometimes but not always followed by a feeling of guilt, can we find the basis for these facts in human nature itself?

THE BASIS IN HUMAN NATURE

Many have sought to establish the proposition that man has a "moral instinct" which, if not interfered with, would impel him to moral conduct; and which, if inhibited for any cause, would occasion distress. If this were true, it would go far toward yielding an understanding of guilt feelings.

But the great variety in the codes themselves, to which we have called attention, seems to block this road of inquiry. If man had the unlearned tendency to perform certain specific acts of a moral character, it would be reasonable to expect the codes themselves to be uniform for all societies. Probably no one now would seriously maintain that this is the case.

Finding it a rather fruitless inquiry to hunt for a moral instinct, it has been more common in recent times to lay hold upon the so-called native desire for approval and the corresponding dread of disapproval; and to trace the sense of guilt to this source. It can hardly be denied that many appear to act from such a motive, especially in childhood; and it may well be true that a measure of it mingles with our motives always. But granting as much as may be true in this respect, does it get to the roots of the matter to say that a sense of guilt is internalized social disapproval? Observe where some of the difficulties lie.

For one thing, the work of the Gestalt psychologists has undermined any claim to the effect that satisfaction and annoyance provide a sufficient ground for understanding of human motivation. Whether or not one accepts the Gestaltist position that behavior results from inner tensions, is partly beside the point. Their experimental work makes it clear that under some conditions even "the animal" responds with a kind of behavior which brings "annoyance," in order to reach its goal. But if "the animal" must choose between the "annoyance" of a certain response, and the "annoyance" of remaining as he is, that fact seems to compel us to acknowledge that even "the animal" has some ability to discriminate.

Again, we have to reckon with the apparent fact that some individuals violate the code and have no apparent sense of guilt about it. Whether there may be an unrecognized sense of guilt in many instances, is a question that still is to be considered. But if it is true that one sometimes violates the code and has no conscious sense of guilt in consequence, it could hardly be maintained very seriously that undifferentiated social approval weighs heavily in all cases.

Once more, when it is urged that guilt feelings are a reaction to social disapproval, it is always necessary to go further and ask whose disapproval was dreaded. For it is a commonplace fact that different groups in modern society have differing standards. This requires us to admit that the individual has something to do with selecting the group whose approval he will seek and whose disapproval he will avoid. But in that case, the pivot on which the act turns is in the individual, and not outside him in society.

For such reasons we are convinced that if we seek to find in human nature itself a basis for the guilt feeling, we must look beyond either a specific "moral instinct," or the internalizing of social disapproval.

We suggest that the inquiry should be pointed, rather, in the direction of man's *capacity for moral discrimination.* Let it be said immediately that this does not refer to any supposed native tendency to regard particular acts as good or bad. On the contrary, we take it for granted that an individual will be taught in his own society what that society regards as good or bad. We refer, rather, to the capacity for sorting things intellectually and emotionally into classes, and considering one in a favorable light while the other is viewed in an unfavorable manner. It is the *capacity* for this sorting out, which is meant.

The capacity itself exists in normal individuals, but *how* it sorts will vary from one culture to another. Both points are illustrated in a story told by a returned naval chaplain who had served in the South Seas. The men of his ship were often ashore on a certain island where it was the custom for the native women to bathe naked at the beach. The sailors would gather a short distance from the shore, watch the bathers, and engage in uproarious laughter.

The native women, scandalized, took the matter to the chief and he in turn went to the naval commander. The latter, sympathetic with the native people, said to the chief, "We'll soon stop that. We'll build a stockade of trees so that the women may bathe in privacy."

But the chief instantly replied, "No, not do that. Tell men to look is good. To laugh is not good." The officer took the chief at his word, told his men what had happened, and all trouble on this score ceased. The standards for the two groups in the matters of "looking" and "laughing" were different, but they quickly found common ground in their shared capacity for moral discrimination.

Another way of regarding the capacity for moral discrimination is to say that the human individual has the ability and the disposition to stand above himself, view himself as if he were an object, and pass deeply emotional judgment upon himself in such contrasted terms as good or bad, worthy or unworthy, right or wrong, decent or indecent, and many another such pair, each profoundly colored with feeling. *What* in himself he will so regard is furnished him by parents, religion, society. *That* he does it seems to be an ultimate in human nature. And the fact that he does this has priority in importance over the material which he uses in doing it, in this sense: since the code surrounding him is not uniform for all groups, he himself must select *what* he shall use as the ground for his own moral discrimination concerning himself.

RESPONSIBILITY AND GUILT

The human being, having the capacity and disposition to approve or condemn himself in terms of moral discrimination, is no isolated monad. He exists within his groups, those groups having a past and a future, a history and a destiny. He is part of the moving stream of life, pushed from behind by his heredity and environment, whatever these may be; while he himself pushes on upon those whose ancestors he will be.

In this dynamic linkage of generations which we call heredity, a particular individual stands at a given moment, let it be supposed, as one who has violated the code. But it is not as if he had acted *de novo,* like some creature dropped full-grown into the world with his first day before him. All the push of his own peculiar heredity is behind him. He acts, again let us suppose, in violation of the code. It may be that afterward misfortune overtakes him, dogs him, breaks him, and seems to pursue his children after him. Who, now, is responsible for what?

In the two preceding lectures we sought to show how acute that question becomes in the ongoing stream of life. Here it will be better to illustrate it from the clinic, where that linkage of the generations seems to walk in at the door with every patient.

Inez Miller was the third of a family of seven children. Each of the first three children had a different father, and Inez' mother had not been married to any of the three men. After Inez' birth her mother married, the husband being still another man. Inez did not know that she was illegitimate until she was eleven years of age; but she did sense that in some way her family was different from others, for her mother had no such callers as other girls' mothers had.

The stepfather was a drunkard, and the mother became an invalid, spending most of her days in a hospital. But from time to time she would leave the hospital for brief intervals, return home, become pregnant, and bear another child, until as we have said the family came to include seven children.

Inez stopped school before she had finished high school, feeling compelled to work for wages to help support the family. But inwardly she rebelled; for the discovery that she had been born out of marriage had shaken her, and now as she worked for wages she realized that all her earnings went to help care for a new baby born of one who was not her own father.

She stopped work and married. But in the marriage she had little to give her husband, because of the basis on which the marriage itself had been entered. After she had been married several years and was pregnant, she discovered that her husband had syphilis.

So she divorced her husband and struggled to care for her little girl, who had been born after the divorce. It was a difficult time; but she got a good job, and eventually married again, the second husband being a man who worked at the same plant. This marriage was happy, and things seemed to be going well. But Inez felt insecure in every relationship. And whatever the occasion, she could not talk of her own life without tears. Meanwhile her daughter Anna, some ten years of age, has become a silent child, holding aloof from companions of her own age, and failing in school. Who, now—we ask again—is responsible for what in this tangled web of circumstances? We could think of that question from Anna's point of view, for she is beginning to fail in living. But rather we now think of it from the point of view of the mother, Inez. Is *she* responsible for Anna's failure?

Perhaps that is the dimly understood but intensely felt problem which brings her in search of help. It is evident from the start of the interviews that the questions which cause her such distress do not lie in the realm of logic and finely calculated justice. Who, indeed, if he were called upon to sit as judge, could say even to his own satisfaction how far Inez is responsible for what is happening in Anna, and how much goes back to social heredity over which Inez had no control whatever?

If she is to find a solution it must be in the realm of feeling. That solution is still in the making, and we do not know what it will be. But she can stand to us now as representing a great number of persons who, confronting the intricate problems of responsibility and having the disposition to judge themselves in terms of moral discrimination, may tend to take one or the other of two general attitudes toward themselves unless they can come to a better solution.

On the one hand, an individual may tend to take the whole responsibility on himself, as if he were guilty of everything, heredity and all. In that event the sense of guilt often becomes overpowering, a crushing load which one cannot bear, and under which he breaks down.

On the other hand, one may tend to abandon all sense of responsibility, and put the burden of it elsewhere, anywhere. Edmund, illegitimate son of Gloucester, expressed this kind of thought when he said,

When we are sick in fortune,—often the surfeits of our own behaviour,—we make guilty of our disasters the sun, the moon, and the stars, as if we were villains on necessity, fools by heavenly compulsion, knaves, thieves, and treachers by spherical predominance, drunkards, liars, and adulterers by an enforc'd obedience of planetary influence, and all that we are evil in, by a divine thrusting on.[1]

In other words, unless a better way can be found one may utilize the whole-or-none type of reaction in the face of staggering problems of responsibility; either he may take it all on himself, holding himself guilty beyond all that logic or justice would require; or he may scuttle all responsibility, standing by to see whether the ship will sink, worm-eaten as it is with the sins of other men.

DISPROPORTION BETWEEN FACT AND FEELING

The all-or-none type of reaction in the face of responsibility may throw light on the frequent disproportion between guilt as fact and guilt as feeling, to which attention has already been called. Very often one commits an act commonly regarded as a serious breach of the code, but appears to have no sense of guilt. A notable and rather extreme instance is that of a young girl who, according to newspaper accounts, killed two members of her family and shot another; but during every kind of examination by police, before a judge, and by doctors, displayed no sign of emotion, and gave no evidence whatever of any sense of guilt.

There are certain extreme conditions in which the sense of guilt appears to be completely lacking. One is the "psychopathic personality," a person well-known in psychiatric practice and in courts of law. In general the psychopathic person is described as one who is emotionally immature, who does not learn by experience in ways such as other persons ordinarily do, and who appears to accept no responsibility for his own acts. He is a familiar figure in criminology; he seems to reverse the normal social relations, and would have the entire world accommodate itself to him. He appears to have no sense of right and wrong, no sense of guilt, and no remorse.[2]

There is also a group of well-known "paranoid" reactions in which the individual locates all faults, mistakes, and sins, outside of himself. If overtaken by misfortune, it is likely he can tell you precisely how the event came about. He will stoutly and unceasingly maintain, for example, that he has been the victim of a plot; others, quite specifically named, have leagued together against him; and so on. He seems to be completely incapable of admitting or even sensing that he himself might have been at fault.

In complete contrast to psychopath or paranoid ways of reacting to responsibility by getting rid of it, and thereby at least consciously getting rid of guilt feelings, there is that large group of persons who are weighed down by a sense of guilt, but who can give to others no reason sufficient to account for the intensity of the suffering.

There are the overscrupulous, for example, who are distressed by a trifle. They are in torment over a peccadillo, or they even imagine some mistake they might have committed, and brood over it, fearful that they *may* have done it. This person is said to be a rather familiar figure in the Roman Catholic confessional.[3]

Again, in some of the many forms of depression, individuals may show every sign of keenest distress, speaking of their great guilt and deploring it; and yet may be unable to point to anything of apparently great consequence which they have done. They make no attempt to place the responsibility elsewhere; *they* are guilty, they say; they will be punished, and they deserve it, they assure us. But they seem unable to tell us *what* they have done to merit such condemnation, except vaguely to say that it was unpardonable, and there is no hope for them now or hereafter.

In their extreme forms all these plainly are abnormal—psychopath and paranoid, or those with obsessions of guilt such as the overscrupulous and the depressed. Such persons are ill, in one manner or another, and in numerous cases unfit for the ordinary responsibilities of living. But they represent types of reaction which are often seen in less extreme forms.

And as a whole these reactions to responsibility for the moral code raise the question whether we can reasonably expect to get to the roots of the sense of guilt by confining ourselves to the level of man's rational thought. Must we go beyond the rational and into the realm of feelings? This appears to be the case; for it looks as if one is entitled to make the generalization that the more serious the sense of guilt, the wider is the gap between that sense of guilt and the specific infraction with which it is consciously associated. That is, in proportion as one is incapable of holding himself accountable for a serious breach of the moral code, he is not thinking rationally, but the processes that go on are of a different character. And by the same token, in proportion as one holds himself to have incurred vast guilt for a minor breach of the code, the intellectual factors in moral judgment are impaired, and other factors in personality have taken over.

What light then is to be found from those clinical experiences and researches which seek to discover whether the roots of the sense of guilt are in the area of feeling and emotion?

GUILT AS FEELING

Certain facts as to man's physical nature need to be taken into account at the outset in this connection. The human individual has two great nervous systems. The more primitive of the two is called the autonomic or vegetative nervous system. It has three divisions. One of these, the cranial, is concerned chiefly with nutrition. The second, the sympathetic, is chiefly concerned with the preservation of the individual under dangers, such as in combat. The third division, the sacral, is concerned primarily with reproduction. This autonomic system is believed to be the older of the two main systems in origin, is largely divorced from voluntary control, and its functions have to do with the preservation of the individual and of the race.

The second of the two great systems is the cerebrospinal, which is the seat of voluntary action, and is responsible for the individual's two-way communication with the physical and social environment, for his adjustment to new situations, and for the higher processes of thought such as the use of abstract ideas, reasoning, and so on. This system is believed to be less primitive than the autonomic, that is, to have developed later in the history of the race.

The autonomic, the older and more primitive of the two systems, is the physical seat of the emotions. Research has shown that the primitive emotions, such as pain, fear, rage, and hunger, not only involve activity in the autonomic system but that these emotions with their bodily changes very quickly spread into the cerebrospinal system, tending to divert the rational and voluntary activity of the latter into more primitive channels, having the preservation of the individual and the race as the instinctive goal.[4]

Thus when a situation is perceived by an individual as either an opportunity or a threat, not only is his instinctive reaction to it an emotional one, but it is made almost instantly as well. "Without thinking," or "quicker than thought," as we say, all the resources of the body are marshalled at the primitive level for the gratification or protection of the self.

But it is not enough merely to see that the mature individual, or even the child, first responds emotionally to an opportunity or a threat and afterward reflects upon what he felt or did. These emotional reactions begin at birth, or perhaps even in the womb. Long before he is capable of reflection, long before he can utter or understand one word of speech, an infant has already had a rich emotional experience, running the full gamut of love, sense of security, satiety, contentment, anxiety, pain, fear, rage, hunger, hate, and so forth. And long before he can begin to learn the moral code of his group, he has already experienced the complex emotions connected with being accepted and loved, or rejected and subtly hated.

It will be recalled that we spoke of the capacity in human beings for moral discrimination, a capacity in virtue of which the individual is disposed to stand above himself and pass judgment upon himself. It must be seen now, in addition, that by the time one begins to be conscious of a self upon which judgment is passed, the self of which he is beginning to be conscious has already, on the whole, been accepted or rejected, loved or hated however subtly, by the persons most closely related to him in infancy, and has formulated patterns of response.

In consequence there come to be, as it were, two strata in the developing personality. One is built up out of the emotional experiences of infancy; this structure is essentially composed of feelings which arose from being loved or hated, and from responding to that love or hostility as the case may be.

The other stratum, if we may call it that, is more open to conscious awareness. It has made large use of the higher mental processes. It has incorporated as much of the moral code as was taught to a given individual. The growing person early becomes capable of reasoning about right and wrong, carries a picture of the judgment others have passed upon him, and eventually becomes capable of passing judgment upon his own actions in moral terms such as good or bad, and so on.

But always there is, as it were, a slumbering volcano of primitive emotions underneath, ready to be touched off into unreasoning activity by any threat to the self. When it has been so touched off, the result often is some violation of the moral code. In that event it appears to be true that the presence or absence of a sense of guilt, and the intensity of the feeling about that particular thing, are governed not so much by rational considerations connected with the specific act, as they are by the underlying structure of more primitive feelings.

What, then, is the nature or character of this underlying structure of primitive feelings?

SEQUENCE AND STRATA

In getting at the question it is necessary to call attention to the fact that emotions tend to arise in a sequence such that when one emotion is aroused another related one is likely also to be stirred. That conception, of course, is very old and grows out of common observation. But in modern depth psychology this common-sense observation has been refined to the point where it is possible to start with certain feelings whose existence is rather obvious, and thence work back to other feelings whose existence is *not* obvious.

Some of the findings as to sequence of emotions are relevant both as to the sense of guilt as such, and also as to the character of the feelings which go into the make-up of the more primitive stratum of personality.

Thus anxiety and guilt are regarded in clinical work as being intimately associated, so much so that when anxiety exists a sense of guilt is inferred. Similarly hostility and guilt are found in clinical experience to be closely associated; for example, hate impulses may suggest the existence of both anxiety and guilt, the hate impulses being a cover for both.

Now if these two conceptions of strata of personality and sequence of emotions are combined, the result suggests that two layers of guilt may be present in one person: a more superficial sense of guilt connected with some infraction of the code, and a deeper sense of guilt arising from primitive levels of emotional experience. In the event the underlying guilt sense is strong, the more superficial sense of guilt may, as it were, tap the underlying volcano; or, to change the figure, may set off an avalanche of feeling out of all proportion to the stone that dislodged it.

Dr. Ernest Jones suggests that stratification holds true of anxiety and hostility, as well as guilt.[5] His thought may be represented in oversimplified form by the following diagram:

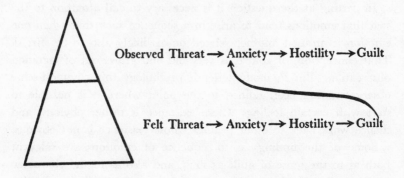

Observed Threat → Anxiety → Hostility → Guilt

Felt Threat → Anxiety → Hostility → Guilt

The details of any such conception must, of course, remain open to correction in the light of continuing research. But in this form there is at least a suggestion as to: (1) two strata in emotional experience, one being open to conscious awareness and reflection, the other a more primitive type of feeling for which an individual can give no explanation to himself; (2) a possible sequence of emotions at each level; (3) the possibility that a deeper sense of guilt may underlie and set off a more superficial anxiety and hostility; and (4) the possibility that each of the conscious states named may grow out of a much deeper one of kindred nature.

GUILT FEELING IN DYNAMIC RELATIONSHIPS

If the deepest and most primitive guilt feelings in the life history of an individual grow out of an equally deep anxiety and hostility, we must seek for the setting in which such a sequence of primitive emotions has its origin. In the simplest possible terms it can be said at once that such a sequence of primitive emotions has its origin in the most dynamic relationships. As observed in the preceding lecture, the most dynamic relationships are such as child to mother and mother to child, child to father and father to child, child to sibling (brother or sister), and so on. Within these most dynamic relationships the emotional experience of an individual child begins; and it begins, as we have just been saying, at the most primitive level, before self-consciousness emerges, before reflection is possible, before discrimination and evaluation are possible, before the code is taught.

In the present state of our knowledge of the primitive levels of emotional experience, there are many gaps yet to be filled in. But research based on clinical material has already thrown much light on the ways in which elemental feelings of guilt originate in certain of the most important of the dynamic relationships. This is notably the case with the child to father relationship, the child to mother relationship, and the child to sibling relationship. Some of the results may be pointed out, with other results still to be mentioned in later connections.

All possible knowledge concerning the child to father relationship has been sought by Freud and his followers, who have correspondingly stressed its importance. He and his orthodox disciples have not only held that the complicated structure of feelings originating in one's infancy is determinative for that person's later life; they have also held that the nature of one's later sense of guilt depends upon his earlier relationship with his father.

When stripped of its peculiar Freudian verbosity, the description of the process as the Freudian sees it runs along such lines as these. The infant, helpless and anxious, depends upon his mother, loves her because she satisfies his needs, and wishes to possess her wholly so that he may have her to himself. The father is felt to be a rival, a threat to such a wish, and the very young child resents the father's place with the mother, feeling an elemental hostility toward him as a thwarter whom he hates.

But any expression of hostility toward the father is promptly frowned upon, forbidden, punished, and abhorred; with the result that even the impulses toward such expressions of hostility cannot get up into full, conscious view. The instant they begin to emerge they are pushed down—"repressed"—with accompanying intense feelings of guilt. This feeling of guilt is, itself, so painful that it cannot be admitted into full consciousness; and yet it is insistently felt, so much so that one also dimly feels the necessity of punishing himself to "atone" for his wrong.

The Freudian conceptions when fully elaborated abound with detailed notions and descriptions of unconscious processes which tax the patience and overtax the credulity of any except a Freudian. We have no concern with, and little interest in, the fine points of Freudian theory. But it must be seen as a point of major significance that the man who has dealt the most courageously with the neurotic by-products of modern civilization has traced so large a share of these ills to the relationship between a child and his father. That will bear pondering in any man's philosophy.

Furthermore, the Freudian line of reasoning, however bizarre in its particulars, has brought a better understanding of one of the strangest of all human capacities, the capacity of man to punish himself without conscious motive for it. We shall return to this subject in the next lecture.

As research went forward with the purpose of uncovering the most primitive emotional experiences of the individual, it became apparent that the Freudian approach, whatever its values, was extremely one-sided in that it bent every fact to fit into the child to father relationship. A more realistic reading of the facts brought to light in the clinic by workers with no Freudian axe to grind made it increasingly evident that the child to mother relationship must be considered in its own right, whatever the manner in which the father fitted into the picture. We may then fairly speak of a second general line of research which has to do with the child to mother relationship. This is not, however, so much a specific line of research as it is a body of facts that has emerged from the experience of the clinic.

It has been found in the clinic that some of the most devastating guilt feelings have their source in what is known as maternal rejection. Maternal rejection is a tragically frequent experience, affecting both mother and child.

We may summarily describe the kind of situation out of which it often arises. A girl growing to womanhood, and having the natural impulse to mate, is taught that her highest privilege is to be a mother and that her supreme obligation is to love her children. The unloving mother is held up as the acme of evil, a violator of nature and a transgressor against God. But in point of actual fact a pregnancy is often very far from being welcome. The situation of the unmarried mother obviously may arouse great distress over the approaching birth. And there are numerous circumstances within marriage, in which the birth of a child may be most unwelcome. There may already be more children than can be properly cared for. The time may seem unfortunate because the mother is unwell, or the husband is out of work; or for any among scores of reasons a particular child may be anything but emotionally desired and accepted.

But the sense of guilt because of having such feelings is often too painful to admit, and it may be pushed back from conscious view without being frankly recognized for what it is. In such an event some form of hostility from mother to child may be expected. The mother may openly express her hostility toward the child, being constantly dissatisfied with anything he does or is; and in such a case life becomes a constant conflict between mother and child, often with such refinements of cruelty as Dante could never have imagined.

Or, instead of being openly hostile, the mother may become oversolicitous for the child, as if to atone for her own feeling toward him. She may overprotect him, and tie him to her in subtle bondage so that his own growth is prevented and he cannot break out of the web so "tenderly" spread around him. He for his part in every probability will secretly hate the mother, perhaps recognizing the hatred or perhaps not; but in either event carrying a sense of guilt arising from the hatred. So hate often begets hate, and guilt in one generation begets guilt in the next, within the family itself, unless the cycle can be broken.

The term "maternal rejection" usually refers to feelings that develop in the mother at or near the time of a child's birth and infancy. But the essential structure of the emotions involved and some of the ramifications are shown in the following case where, apparently, rejection by the mother took form when the child was several years of age.

When we first meet him, Winston A is a boy some fifteen years of age, an invalid, confined to bed, emaciated in body with an apathetic look in his eyes, frequently complaining of great pain. Mrs. A, his mother, is a woman of intelligence and breeding. They live in a simple home without luxuries, for the income is not large and much of it has had to go, year after year, into bills for doctors, medicines, and hospital service. The mother denies herself all comforts and all diversions in order to care for Winston. For nearly eight years she has done little more than attend him in his suffering; she takes him to doctors, visits him in hospitals, or when he is at home prepares special foods for him, serves his wants, and sees that his medicine is taken regularly day and night.

Winston's invalidism dates from his eighth year, when he fell from a ladder and hurt his back. He had not been doing well in school, and since he did not recover promptly from the fall, he had to be taken out of school; and he never grew well enough to return.

His trouble proved difficult to locate and treat. Doctors seemed able to do little for him. They could find no physical basis for the pain of which he spoke, nor for his inability to walk. They could not even agree upon a diagnosis, and Winston was treated for one ailment after another, but without improvement; meanwhile he grew weaker. A doctor would treat the boy for a time and become hopeful of recovery or at least of improvement. But only after Winston had been an invalid for years was it observed that whenever a physician would become optimistic about Winston and begin to speak of the possibility that he might walk again, Mrs. A would immediately insist with great vigor that Winston's case was hopeless; and she would change doctors.

When he was about fifteen, Winston was placed under the care of a psychiatrist, and the life story of mother and son began to be put together. Mrs. A, the mother, was the daughter of a minister of considerable standing in the community. As a girl she greatly admired her father, who became to her a model of all that a man should be. She had married a man of substantial character, but beneath her in social standing and ability, and she had little genuine respect for her husband. Four children, boys, were born of this marriage before Winston came. Each of these four boys as he grew old enough left high school before graduation and went to work in some trade. Secretly Mrs. A carried a deep disappointment not only in her marriage but also in each of the four boys, as it became evident that none of them would ever fulfill what had now become the deepest ambition of her life, that a son of hers should be a minister like her own father.

About ten years after the birth of the fourth child Winston was born. The mother's hopes were now set on this lad who should become her minister. As soon as he was able to talk she began to instill the idea into him, saying that *this* son should be molded to her heart's desires. But the boy proved to be below average in intelligence, learned slowly at home, and quickly had difficulties in school. Before the time of the fall from the ladder even the boy's mother was compelled to recognize that Winston could not take even an elementary education, and once more the frustration of her hopes and ambitions loomed in her way.

Precisely what took place in the mother's own feelings remains obscure in many respects, for Mrs. A herself was not a patient. But during the course of a long treatment of Winston and the consequent interviews with the mother, it became obvious to the psychiatrist that death wishes toward the son, at the time of the fall from the ladder, had come so near the surface in the mother as to terrify her. Then as if to atone for the guilt of such dimly recognized feelings, she had become a martyr, giving herself to unceasing care of her sick son; and once having found this compromise solution for the problem of her own hatred and guilt, she must keep Winston an invalid lest this one prop, her continuing atoning martyrdom, be removed.

Winston, for his part, was deprived of genuine maternal love, but clung to the substitute for it which was given him through his mother's solicitude. If that were taken from him quickly, there was nothing to put in its place. Remaining an invalid kept his mother at his call, and insured him this kind of "love."

But his own hatred for his mother, as dimly recognized as was hers toward him, was even more intense than hers, if that is possible. His hatred could express itself for years only by keeping her a slave to him in his illness. As the treatment went on during separation from the mother, some of the hostility toward her began to come out, but the boy was frightened by the intensity of his feelings, and never succeeded in expressing it fully. A similar hostility often comes out much more completely in other comparable cases, with a tremendous discharge of emotion.

After months of treatment in separation from the mother, Winston left the hospital, walking alone, and was able to take simple jobs. Many details obviously have to be omitted in relating the case. We still are left with the question of whether Mrs. A's relationship with her father may have been a precipitating factor in her own relationships to her husband and children. That question cannot be answered since, as was said, Mrs. A herself was not a patient. But the salient points given illustrate hostility and guilt in the mother-son relationship, and exemplify the paradox that mother and child may be bound together by ties of hatred which neither mother nor child alone can break.

Primitive levels of emotional experience have been explored more fully, perhaps, with reference to child to father and child to mother relationships than with any other of the most dynamic relationships. But the relationships between siblings have received a share of attention, and some of the work is significant in connection with our inquiry, since it shows the very early emergence of guilt feelings along with hostility toward a brother or sister.

What is known as "sibling rivalry" is, of course, a common experience in family life, as when one child feels himself displaced by another. The jealousy, bitterness, and poorly concealed animosity that often arise between the children of one family are evident to any observant person. In some instances the behavior of a child in such a situation becomes so difficult as to require skilled treatment.

Cases involving sibling rivalry in some form come in considerable numbers to certain types of clinics. It has been found that a specially devised play technique, properly controlled, gives opportunity for a child's hostility toward his mother or toward another child in the family to be expressed toward dolls. The dolls may represent, for example, the mother and a younger child whom the older child regards as having displaced him in the mother's affections.

Under these conditions the primitive impulses may be expressed with vigor and even ferocity, as when a child seizes a celluloid doll representing the new baby, and chews the doll to bits. A special toy known as the "amputation doll" is used when obtainable; this type of doll not only can be dismembered by a child if he so desires, but can also be put together again by him if he wishes. Whatever the type of doll used, a child's hostility toward some member of the family often finds expression in such primitive ways as by biting it, crushing it, dismembering it, burning it, and so on.

In a series of controlled experiments, using the "play technique" with children disturbed by sibling rivalry situations, David M. Levy found that guilt feelings arose in children of three and four in connection with their primitive hostility toward the mother or the sibling.[6] He reports that when once the hostile behavior is set in motion it tends to run according to a typical pattern. After the attack on the object, during which he releases hostility, a child was found to follow one or more of three general lines of what Levy called "self-redeeming" behavior. He might begin to punish himself in some manner; and in the experimental situation it was observed that the amount of self-punishment was equal to the hostility displayed. Or a child might attempt to make good the damage he had caused, as by restoring the injured object to its former state. Or a child might defend himself by such measures as lies, evasions, self-justification for what he had done, and so on. These findings are of especial interest in that they appear to demonstrate experimentally the emergence of a primitive guilt feeling in connection with primitive hostility, as early as three and four years of age.

We have been considering the possibility that the most primitive feelings of guilt may originate very early in an individual's life, within certain dynamic relationships such as those between parents and child and those between siblings. We must now ask whether the case of the psychopath is an exception.

The psychopath, it may be repeated, appears to have no sense of guilt when he violates the code. For example, he may lie, swindle, cheat, deviate widely in his sex conduct, steal, or kill in cold blood; and apparently he has not the slightest twinge of conscience. But is the appearance in keeping with the deepest reality? Does he, in fact, have an especially deep sense of guilt which is unusually well covered even from himself?

The question cannot be answered with entire satisfaction at present. To begin with, the label "psychopath" may itself be a bad one, covering diverse patterns of behavior which should never have been lumped together. Nevertheless it remains in use. Again, psychiatrists themselves are not agreed as to the way or ways in which one becomes a psychopath. Was he born with a constitution different from that of "normal" persons, or is his lack of moral self-judgment due to his own experience from infancy onward?

A majority of psychiatrists, it is said,[7] are of the opinion that psychopathy is inborn. If this is so, certain persons who are not deficient in intelligence are born defective in the capacity for moral judgment, especially moral self-judgment. It has sometimes been said that they were born morally insane, or morally imbecile.

But to some psychiatrists this is not convincing,[8] and certain objections raised against it are relevant here. It is pointed out that deep and careful work with younger psychopaths *does* reveal an unconscious sense of guilt in a sufficient number of cases to make it appear highly probable that it exists in others also.

Further, it is said that in the early experience of a psychopath such a person, typically, has never had any relationships with any individuals whom he could fundamentally and thoroughly trust. Sooner or later he has always been "double-crossed," and he retaliates by "double-crossing" everyone else.

The "double-crossing" may take place in the family, as in the case of parents who are inconsistent in the emotional relationships with a child. The child's response then may become a technique for hiding feelings of hate and guilt lest he be punished more. He learns to live by his wits. Fundamentally his parents have no code, although they may profess one; and their child grows up without a code.

The punishment which the psychopath often visits upon himself directly or indirectly is taken, in this view, as a symptom of unconscious guilt. If this general position should prove to be better founded than the one which regards psychopathy as inborn defectiveness, the psychopath's apparent lack of guilt feeling would appear to have its origin in primitive emotional experience, within dynamic relationships that were defective.

But whatever the eventual conclusions as to the psychopath, other considerations which we have briefly presented point to the emergence of a primitive sense of guilt, early in an individual's life, in connection with primitive anxiety and hostility within the relationships between child and parent and those between siblings.

It is to be recognized again that work of this character must remain open to rigorous correction in the light of accumulating clinical experience. In such an area as this, dogmatism has no rights; the facts as they pile up must speak for themselves. The study of emotional experience during the early years of life has already proved revolutionary; its full implications are yet to be seen. But in the present state of our knowledge it appears certain that the sense of guilt in the maturer years of an individual's life cannot be seen in its true import unless we also reckon with that person's emotional experience during the earliest years of his life within his most intimate relationships.

However, it is not necessary to rest the case at this point alone. It is possible, as it were, to cross-examine our evidence as to the nature of man's deeper sense of guilt from still another angle. We are to do that in the next lecture.

THE OUTCROPPINGS OF GUILT

THE FEELING of guilt, when that feeling issues out of the deeper strata of the personality, is one of the most painful of all human experiences. The suffering, being the result both of hurt and terror, is so intense that it cannot be borne for long periods of time without deterioration of some sort. If the feeling of guilt were admitted to full consciousness, the true nature of the self would become evident, and the consequent destruction of self-esteem would be unbearable. The human organism seems capable of enduring anything in the universe except a clear, complete, fully conscious view of one's self as he actually is.

As if sensing intuitively that it cannot bear to gaze open-eyed and unaided into the depth of its own being, the organism has elaborated numerous devices for protecting itself against a complete view of the self as it is, otherwise the self might become split into two selves, thus losing selfhood, unity of consciousness, sense of continuation as one being, and, in the deepest sense, life itself. It is not to be supposed that this is rhetorical speech; for, as we shall see, if the deepest sense of guilt is not adequately dealt with there may come to be a cleavage of personality so radical as to destroy the unity of the self.

Since deeper guilt feelings are so intolerable, we cannot expect that they will be exposed to the full view of other persons even so much as to the full view of the one in whom they exist. The deepest sense of guilt is shielded from one's own view, and is screened off from the gaze of others by protecting devices and by the discharge of other more socially acceptable feelings.

These more manifest feelings may be thought of as outcroppings of layers or strata that are still deeper in the self. These more readily observable feelings signify that the individual has worked out a precarious balance between conflicting elements that lie deeper within the self. By means of this delicate balancing of conflicting trends within, one can "get by" a little longer without profoundly changing the deepest structure of the personality. We thus have another of the paradoxes of human nature: a sense of guilt in its more obvious forms of expression may serve the purpose of blocking a deeper reconstruction of the self.

There are several kinds of outcropping symptoms of guilt which may be related in one manner or another to a deeper, more obscure sense of guilt. It is the purpose in this lecture to consider some of these outcropping symptoms, and to indicate some of the ways in which they may arise out of deeper elements within the self. It seems preferable to take up the latter point first.

GUILT, ANXIETY, AND HOSTILITY

We must renew the mention of two conceptions to which reference was made in the last lecture, namely, sequence and strata of emotions. It was remarked that guilt, anxiety, and hostility appear to be related to each other in such a way that when one of the trio appears we are prepared to expect the others. One is reminded of the roles taken by the three witches in *Macbeth*. In that drama, when we hear one of the three witches speaking we know that she is telling only one part of a total story which the trio are waiting to rehearse. In order to get the story as a whole, we must wait until the other two have also spoken. The case is somewhat similar as concerns guilt, anxiety, and hostility. When one of the three appears, the others are probably lurking in the background.

But we have no certainty as to which of the three will first meet the observant eye. The symptoms which are most apparent at the surface of living in the case of a given person might be guilt, or anxiety, or hostility. The others might lie out of sight, their depth and their strength unknown. For such reasons we may use another figure in order to call attention again to the conception of strata within the personality. The dynamics of the relationship between guilt, anxiety, and hostility might be compared to a spiral, made like a corkscrew and embedded in some object; we know there is more of the spiral beneath the surface, and we know it finally comes to a point, but we do not know how deep down into the object one would be required to go in order to reach the point of origin.

It could be imagined, furthermore, that on the rounds of this spiral, guilt, anxiety, and hostility succeed one another time after time; so that if one thought of the process from the point of view of its origin it would seem as if the guilt, anxiety, and hostility were emerging from unknown depths; and if one thought of the process from the point of view of investigating it, it would remind him of burrowing deeper and ever deeper into the object until, if we were wise enough, we might eventually arrive at the primal source of the guilt, anxiety, and hostility within a particular individual. In either event perhaps one can visualize a long and destructive process by which guilt, anxiety, and hostility arise out of yet deeper guilt, anxiety, and hostility, each kindling and stirring up the other.

With these rude comparisons in mind as a way of reminding ourselves that the sense of guilt, or the feeling of anxiety, or the feeling of hostility may exist beneath the surface as well as on the surface, and that the superficial may be dynamically related to the deeper, we take up a more specific consideration of anxiety.

ANXIETY

The state of apprehensiveness known as anxiety is familiar enough to anyone who has had stage fright, or has been very homesick. It is akin to fear, but is prolonged. It varies in intensity from very mild to acute. In its milder forms it is one of man's most frequent experiences. In its more severe forms it is said to be one of the most common conditions met in medical practice. The physician, of course, seeks to ascertain whether there is a physical basis for the anxiety; but in a great number of cases he finds that the anxiety exists and persists without any ascertainable physical cause.

Anxiety may become chronic, in which case a person may show such characteristic symptoms as irritability, tenseness, general dissatisfaction, sense of fatigue, fear of particular diseases, and so on. There may be acute attacks with a state of panic, in which the patient shows such symptoms as rapid heart, nausea, feeling of choking or suffocating, dizziness or faintness, sense of impending death, and so on.[1] The cause given by the person to account for the anxiety may be very specific, and the occasion for the anxiety, as stated, may be anywhere within a range as wide as life itself. As Jesus observed long ago, one may be anxious as to what he will eat, what he will drink, and what he will wear. He may be anxious over the health of an infant, the failure of a child at school, misfortune in his family, his own physical health, or any other of a thousand things.

In other cases the anxiety may be more vague, a diffuse but severe state of apprehensiveness, in which one is not able to "put his finger" on the cause. Then,

> "We fear, yet know not what we fear,
> But float upon a wild and violent sea.

In anxiety states a feeling of helplessness mingles with that of dread. Disaster, whether definite or vague in its shape, seems impending, yet we cannot lift a finger to avert it, can discover no way to delay it, and feel that in a matter of moments, or hours at most, it will engulf us.

But against *what* is the anxious person helpless? That is the first major point of inquiry concerning anxiety. And here the psychiatrists tend to speak with one voice, however much they may vary in the details of what they say. The real cause of the anxiety is not outside the person but within him. There may, of course, be occasions of concern in the person's circumstances, but the removal or change of the circumstances does not remove the anxiety, for the anxiety then will probably become attached to something else in its place. The occasion may precipitate the anxiety but is not the true cause of it. One may indeed be helpless before the particular occasion of the anxiety, but the anxiety takes on its intensity and its fearful quality because of something within him too dreadful for that particular person to admit to his own conscious view. He is afraid of something within himself which is unacceptable to himself —too horrible, too awful even to think of.

By seizing upon something dreadful outside of himself as the cause of anxiety, one protects himself from the still more dreadful thing within, which he cannot accept, cannot even admit is true. This was shown with striking symbolism in the case of a woman who was morbidly afraid of thunderstorms, with an anxiety so great that upon the mention or even the thought of a storm she would grow agitated and cling to others for reassurance. But it proved that the deeper "storm" which she feared was within herself. She expressed fear that she might kill any person who came in her way. When this fear of what she herself might do was healed, the fear of storms outside herself disappeared.

When we ask what it is within the self that underlies anxiety and is too dreadful to be accepted by the conscious mind, we get answers which at first seem to disagree, but which finally merge into one.

The Freudians, especially in their earlier works, tended to trace anxiety to sex impulses which cannot be accepted by the person in whom they exist. They were much disposed to associate certain manifestations of anxiety with one or another particular practice or impulse, such as masturbation, homosexualism, and so on. Conceptions of this kind regarding the factors underlying anxiety left a deep trace in the early literature, and to a lesser extent a similar trace in common thought. And it can hardly be doubted that in some instances anxiety exists in persons whose sex impulses seem to them too dreadful to be tolerated or recognized for what they are.

But as time has passed, and as clinical experience has broadened, the Freudians themselves are tending to go beneath sex, at least in any narrow sense, and to seek a more profound source of anxiety. Others, psychiatrists working independently and quite outside of Freudian circles, have been engaged in the same attempt, that is, to ascertain the common source which underlies forms of anxiety. The results turn out to be surprisingly alike when due allowance is made for differences in approach and vocabulary. And they are far-reaching in their implications for all human living.

Put in their simplest terms they indicate that anxiety arises chiefly out of hostility.[2] Hostility, here, may be distinguished from aggression. Aggression follows the pattern of attack, but it appears that hostility is stored up with the greatest strength in some of the very persons whose background has taught them to be meek and humble. But such generalizations need to be further examined.

LOVE AND HOSTILITY

Various terms are often used as the general equivalent of hostility, each one signifying some different shade of meaning or intensity of feeling; such as resentment, antagonism, negativism, aggression, hatred, the death wish, and so on.

Hostility is aroused when one is thwarted, that is, when he is prevented from reaching some goal which he wishes to achieve. But life, of course, holds innumerable thwartings for every individual, and the hostilities that result are not of equal significance. Not every kind of hostility is equally productive of anxiety. The hostility which is most fertile in this respect, the hostility that is instantly felt as the gravest threat to the self in whom it exists, is hostility within the most dynamic relationships. The hostility which is felt as the most dangerous is hostility toward the very persons whom one loves the most. Furthermore, the depth of the love which one has toward another appears to be the measure of the hostility which he is capable of feeling toward that person.

It can be said, then, that the deepest anxiety arises out of the hostility that is stirred when love is thwarted. But on the other hand it has to be said at once also that love cannot grow if it is never thwarted in any manner. The apparent contradiction may be understood if we consider more closely what is meant by love, that word which must cover so vast a range of experiences.

Human life by its very nature demands the satisfaction of two great needs, and yet the individual is almost constantly in tension between these two needs. One is the need to identify himself with something greater and stronger than himself, as a means of protecting the self in its littleness against annihilation. The other is the need to become an individual, a person, one who is not submerged, one who can respect himself in his own right, who can choose his own ends for striving, and can pursue those ends without external domination. Our nature being what it is, both needs must be met and kept in some kind of equilibrium if we are to thrive. But again, our nature and our world being what they are, the balance which we may achieve between these needs today is not quite sufficient for tomorrow, as tomorrow the balance will be disturbed again, and another must be worked out.

When the first of these, the need for identification with something greater and stronger than oneself is met, there is a sense of oneness, a feeling of unity with the object. When that oneness exists, the feeling state that suffuses the relationship with warmth, tenderness, and an indescribable sense of well-being, is love. That state itself is so rich with meaning that no one word can ever include it all. It may be a sign of our own emotional poverty that we who speak English must press this one word into service as a symbol for what is, in fact, a galaxy of experiences. For such reasons it is imperative that we free ourselves of any notion that love is always one and the same thing, either in the feelings that comprise it, or in the strength which it has.

Two words for the purpose of bringing out distinctions within love are only a little better than one. But the Greek language, expressing refinements of meaning in this regard which we usually ignore, made good use of the terms Eros and Agape. Again in modern times the distinction has proved highly suggestive in the hands of such men as Nygren,[3] a Swedish theologian, and Otto Rank,[4] a psychiatrist. The terms themselves have a direct bearing on hostility and anxiety.

Eros and Agape are two kinds of love, or two motives in love; for love is not merely feeling, but is action with its resulting feeling as well. Eros is love whose motive is to enhance the status of the self within a relationship. Its characteristic actions are designed to control, dominate, and use the one who is loved. Agape is love whose motive is to enhance the status of the one loved. Its typical actions are designed to liberate the loved one by means of the relationship so that the other may grow and thrive.

The strategy of Eros is emotional encirclement and capture of the loved one. *Sex activity and sex feeling comprise one, but only one, among many manifestations of Eros; it cannot be too strongly emphasized that Eros love is not restricted to sex; neither is sex in its richer manifestations solely a matter of Eros.* Eros, it should be repeated for the sake of clarity, is that love whose motive is enhancing the status of the self by capturing and controlling the loved one, whether the one to be emotionally captured is a child, a mate, a parent, a new acquaintance, or a business prospect. The plea of Eros is, "Come, do my bidding, and you shall gain all that your heart could desire."

The strategy of Agape is not so, neither is its plea the same. That strategy apparently breaks all laws of reason; therefore it is difficult for minds to grasp it, and difficult emotionally to accept it when one loves. Rank has correctly pointed out that as far as we can know, it came into human speech later in history than Eros did. Its strategy is designed to secure emotional oneness with the loved object by means of liberating him. Nor is Agape a business of merely freeing slaves in order to get more faithful retainers. Its favorite field of operation is the most dynamic relationships, such as those between parent and child, husband and wife, and so on. It begins by setting the loved one free, step by step with whatever patient slowness may be required, but always within a relationship which never breaks but only grows stronger as the freedom enlarges. And there must be no mistaking the character of the freedom intended; it is genuine and limitless. The motto of Agape is, "Go, when you wish and where you wish. Do what you will, for I trust you."

As an infant begins life the first love which he has toward another is Eros love, and it is that by the necessities of his situation. But observe that without thwarting of one kind or another, the Eros love which he experiences as his first love cannot grow beyond that Eros love. For the infant's need for oneness is first met biologically by his physical oneness with the mother before birth. But that particular oneness cannot continue to exist much beyond its appointed time, else death will ensue for both mother and child. The oneness must be ruptured if growth is to continue. This inexorable law will brook no exceptions.

And that law which unmistakably governs the relationship between the bodies of the two before birth appears also to govern the emotional relationship between the two after birth; and then later still also to govern the other relationships which the child will eventually enter. The birth of a child thus seems a symbolical foreshadowing of the later human career if life and love are to grow, and not stagnate.

Thus struggle and suffering are inseparably connected with growth toward and into Agape love. The oneness as it exists in a relationship will have to be ruptured and remade on a slightly more mature level if there is to be growth; and this process will have to be repeated again and again if growth is to continue. Each rupture of an existing relationship can mark a new stage, however small a one, in the process of becoming an individual person. The breaking of the oneness brings anguish to mother and child, but it is the anguish without which there can be no growth.

If then we consider the career of the individual from infancy onward, it seems to be impossible for him to move into Agape love without having known Eros love, in which he can gratify his emotional need. It is as if one must be the center of some universe before he can forget himself. If he has never known that experience, he seems forever to pursue it, hungry for affection, but not receiving it because he cannot give it, unable to give it because he never received it. Denied the subsoil of human thriving, he must keep himself the center of his little universe; a center from which he cannot break forth to discover what the universe actually is.

This line of thought concerning two kinds of love and the pain of growing from Eros love toward Agape love now breaks up into a score of channels which one might follow. We shall return to parts of it in later connections and pick them up again for further exploration. But here we are chiefly concerned with the point that thwarting, which is a necessary prelude to growth, arouses hostility within the relationship where love is.

It is well to be under no sentimental illusions as to the depth and intensity of the primitive hostility which is aroused when Eros love, the love seeking to enhance the standing of the self, is thwarted. When Eros love is thwarted, the primitive impulse is to destroy the object whose love was sought.

This primitive hostility toward the object of love, when it cannot be admitted to consciousness and dealt with for what it truly is, is vaguely but powerfully felt as a monstrous danger threatening to destroy one's self. And in fact it *is* just such a threat as that, nothing less. The feeling of threat *is* the anxiety, and the anxiety arises out of what is essentially a moral crisis in the self. But the issue is not brought out into the open; instead, a compromise of some sort is reached in the dim emotional world of the individual. It is as if conscience had sat in moral judgment on the self, and passed sentence of condemnation, but without ever having heard the case. Then it is left for the self, threatened within but deluded by itself as to the true nature of the danger, to begin erecting its defenses against the guilt feeling. But before we consider some of these defenses which are outcropping symptoms it remains to call attention to some further distinctions.

KINDS OF ANXIETY

From several different quarters in modern times emphasis has been laid on two facts: that no human creature can be free from anxiety, and that anxiety is of many kinds. When it comes to analyzing the different kinds of anxiety, however, we do not yet have general agreement.

Consider first some of those who have approached the subject from the vantage point of depth psychology. Freud attached great importance to what he called *Urangst,* or primitive anxiety, due to the shock of birth and the ensuing helplessness. Otto Rank devoted attention to what he called "the trauma of birth." In Jungian thought the discrepancy between the personality which one natively is and the personality which cultural pressures have caused him to try to be, is a source of profound anxiety.

Karen Horney laid stress on a "basic anxiety" which she found peculiarly active in neurotics. This anxiety she describes in the familiar but unavoidable terms: the feeling of being small, helpless, in danger, deserted, in a world bent on cheating one, abusing him, humiliating him, and finally getting rid of him. She insists that this anxiety originates in infancy in the case of those persons who were deprived of warm and genuine parental affection, that is, persons who in earliest life were rejected emotionally.[5]

Consider next a group of persons who have approached the subject of anxiety from the vantage point of theology. These persons, however, are intimately acquainted with the literature of depth psychology and in several instances with clinical experience as well.

Soren Kierkegaard lived before the days of modern depth psychology, but his writings have exerted a strong influence on the theology of the self, and to a considerable extent on depth psychology. Many of his books are concerned with one or another aspect of anxiety. One of these treats of despair, which he calls "the sickness unto death"—a condition inherent in man himself, who cannot attain true selfhood by his own efforts; yet, continuing to assert himself, he misses his only opportunity to become a self, and sinks into still deeper despair. He can only emerge into selfhood within a "synthesis," or relationship with God.[6]

Influenced by Kierkegaard and by Augustine, Reinhold Niebuhr developed the thesis that man is a creature of two dimensions. As finite, he is a part of nature, subject to its laws and its vicissitudes; but as self-conscious, man transcends himself, being capable of viewing himself as object, and thus is a creature of spirit. As part of nature he is limited, as spirit he is above nature and is free. He is in tension between the two, and that tension is his anxiety, which is not sin but tempts to sin. Helpless and insecure, his will overreaches his limitations; he attempts to be what he cannot be, becoming a god in his own eyes. This, his pride, is his sin; and his pride grows from his anxiety.[7]

At still more recent dates, studies of various aspects of anxiety have been continued by Paul Tillich, Rollo May, Wayne E. Oates, and Charles R. Stinnette, Jr.[8]

May, in *The Meaning of Anxiety*, gives a valuable summary of the literature on anxiety up to about 1950, and contributes to the subject by case studies from his own clinical practice. Both May and Tillich distinguish between normal anxiety and abnormal or neurotic anxiety.

Tillich, in *The Courage to Be,* discusses and analyzes normal or "existential" anxiety which is not neurotic but is common to all men simply in virtue of existence as such. He distinguishes three forms of existential anxiety: the anxiety of fate and death, the anxiety of emptiness and meaninglessness, and the anxiety of guilt and condemnation.

The works of Niebuhr and Tillich have exerted a deep influence on modern thought and are often reflected in psychological as well as in theological writings.

Oates, in *Anxiety in Christian Experience,* fuses insights drawn from Biblical thought, psychotherapy, and pastoral counseling. He identifies a number of types of anxiety such as economic anxiety, finitude anxiety, the anxiety of grief, the anxiety of sin, the anxiety of legalism, the anxiety of moral indifference, and the anxiety of the cross, which is the anxiety of the self that must die before it can be raised up to a new, full, and secure life.

In *Anxiety and Faith* Stinnette examines the theological dimension of anxiety and distinguishes three chief types. The first is primary anxiety; this is the anxiety of existence, and arises out of man's freedom. The second is sinful anxiety. It arises out of man's separation from God, with a loss of freedom. The third is neurotic anxiety, arising out of disturbed human relations.

When all these approaches are taken into view it is evident that the term "anxiety" as it has now come to be used covers an extremely wide range of meanings. For present purposes we may distinguish three groups of these meanings. (1) There is normal or existential anxiety. This arises out of the nature of human existence as such, and is the lot of all men as finite creatures. (2) There is abnormal or neurotic anxiety. This is rooted in the unconscious, and is fed by deep emotional disturbances, especially by emotional deprivation in early life. And (3) there is situational anxiety. This is aroused by the realities of some situation which contains a threat to the self. It tends to disappear with the removal of the threat or with the passing of time.

It is not to be supposed that these are three sharply distinct entities. In experience any one form may pass almost imperceptibly into another. Thus prolonged situational anxiety may pass over into a neurotic condition; or a neurotic anxiety may give place to the acceptance of an irreducible minimum of normal anxiety; or some deep apprehensiveness which is put forward as existential anxiety may turn out in fact to be a neurotic anxiety hidden under the philosopher's robe.

We return now to renew the inquiry into the relation between anxiety, hostility, and guilt. We have just observed that an individual may carry any one of many kinds of anxiety. The nature of such anxiety as he carries has much to do with the intensity and duration of the emotions aroused by any specific threat to the self. For example, one person who basically has a strong sense of security and is relatively free from neurotic anxiety, when thwarted can quickly vent his hostility and can almost as quickly pass beyond the incident. Another, already deeply anxious and now threatened afresh at some tender point, may be afraid to express or even to recognize his own hostility. In that event the unexpressed hostility may grow in strength, probably increasing the anxiety still further and at the same time further feeding the sense of guilt.

But whatever the precise nature of the dynamics at work in the human underworld, we have to reckon with the possibility that the sense of guilt, which cannot be faced for what it is, may crop out in the form of symptoms.

SYMPTOMS OF GUILT

We may go on, then, to consider some of the symptoms which may suggest that feelings of guilt are cropping out. It is to be borne in mind that the symptoms of which we are about to speak are an outward ring of defenses protecting the self which has been threatened and is apprehensive over its own status. Little can be accomplished, ordinarily, by a direct attack upon the symptoms themselves; what is required is a deep inward reconstruction and release. In the story of Peter's imprisonment under Herod it is said that when he was set free in the inward part of the prison, he passed through the outer ward, coming at last to the iron gate which led out into the city; and this gate opened, then, of its own accord. So it is with the symptoms of guilt.

Since the symptoms or outcroppings are the protection of the threatened self, it may be useful to view them in several groups, each of which exhibits a more or less typical way of setting up an outward iron gate to defend a self which is threatened from within. Of course it will not be supposed that any one individual will shield himself in all of these ways; the one which he takes appears to be governed by his entire previous life history.

APPEASEMENT

One group of ways by which the threatened self may attempt to make its position more secure may be put under the general head of appeasement. On the whole these are designed to win favor and affection for the self which is in danger. They are intended to make it exceedingly plain that the self has qualities that are lovable; and therefore others ought to treat this self with kindness, consideration, and esteem.

Self-rehabilitation. Nunberg[9] is one among many who have called attention to the fact that when the individual feels insecure because of some inward threat he may seek to reconcile others to himself by means of presents, lavish expenditure, and other similar measures with the general purpose of increasing the affection one will receive from some one person or group.

Excessive generosity is often recognized by common sense as a mark of guilt feeling, but it is not so easily recognized that the scale on which the gifts are made may be an index to the strength of the hostility felt. That hostility may be so great that one unconsciously assumes it must require an impressive present to appease the other who is the object of so much hostility. Thus when Jacob is about to encounter Esau many years after his theft of the latter's birthright, the princely gift which he sends in advance as a greeting is hardly so much a measure of his love toward his brother as it is a gauge of his continuing animosity. Had he been genuinely desirous of enhancing his brother's welfare, it is to be supposed he would have renounced the birthright which he had gained by trickery.

A similar motive can be expressed symbolically. It has recently been reported in news dispatches that a certain man gave the bulk of a rather substantial fortune to an orphans' home. It was also said of him that he spent a large part of the latter forty years of his life bitterly quarreling with the children of his own neighborhood who insisted upon playing on his lawn. The strength of his hostility may well be left to the imagination.

Self-righteousness. The form of appeasement to which we have just referred is an attempt to reconcile the surrounding world to one's self by being exceedingly lovable; there is another form af appeasement which attempts to gain the same general end by being exceedingly good. One who is threatened by forces within himself which he cannot face for what they are, may reinforce his own shaken self-regard by piling up, for others to see, the evidences of his superlative goodness.

By one of the strangest of all anomalies, religion may become a channel of expression for a fierce kind of goodness on the part of persons who are unable to reconstruct their own inner world. There then arises an aggressive professional goodness which may be the guise for a tremendous but unrecognized hostility. This may come about as a personal solution for an otherwise unmanageable hostility in the relations between individuals, as in a family; but there are periods in the history of religion which prove to be especially favorable to the emergence of aggressive goodness as a common form of religious expression. The point that especially concerns us here is the presence of hostility, recognized or unrecognized, in connection with many instances of great emphasis upon a high and rigid moral code.

Zilborg,[10] for example, has remarked that many cases brought to the clinics involve a problem of this nature in the relations between parents and children. There is the parent, father or mother, who makes exacting ethical demands upon his child, demands which are couched in such terms that the child finds it virtually impossible to meet them. Such a child then becomes more and more identified in the parent's eyes as a person who will not obey, or will not observe the common decencies, or is defiant, or whatever kind of transgressor he may be. It is only the more fitting that he should receive the severest punishment, whether that be physical, or the depriving of affection, or whatever else may be visited upon him. The full storm of parental displeasure can then be vented upon a son or daughter with such a character. Zilborg maintains that in many such instances, analysis shows the parent was hostile to such a child before the child's provocative behavior began. But in such circumstances the parent may be reckoned by his acquaintances as an upright man or woman, a person of sterling character who has been grievously disappointed in his black sheep of a child. Thus the father or mother is able, as it were, to appease society for the hatred toward his own child.

The classic example of the self-righteous person is the Pharisee, who represents a period or movement in history which was especially conducive to aggressive goodness as an outlet for tremendous hostility. As a party they had come to being during a time when the Jews as a people had been thwarted as never before, for they had been forced to drink a bitter cup whose dregs were made up of military defeat, the overthrow of their religion, and indignity to their persons. Among them were men who, in their long pondering over the meaning of these things, came to the conviction that the cause of their woes was their neglect of Jehovah's Torah, or law, and that the healing of those ills could come only by the faithful observance of that neglected law. The Pharisees were a party who stood for a stricter and ever stricter observance of that law.

It was said of them in their own day that they did their righteousness in order to be seen of men, and in this we have whatever motive there may have been of appeasing their own world by their own excessive goodness. Unfriendly critics said that when they gave alms they were sure to sound a trumpet in order that their gifts might be made known. When they prayed, it was in full sight of their fellows, in such places as street corners where no one could fail to see. And it was said of them that when they fasted they were at much pains to show a sad countenance in order that no one might possibly mistake them for persons who had any joy of heart left.

The hostility which found its vent through this public, professional expression of loyalty to God has not been quite so commonly recognized, although evidences of it are plain enough. Their antagonisms, however, were quite as evident as their righteousnesses. They despised the "common people," the rabble, the uncleansed folk who either could not or would not keep the finer points of the law and hence in Pharisaic eyes were in a perpetual state of defilement. They despised the Gentiles who knew nothing of Jewish Torah and cared less, and therefore were but dogs fit only to be kicked out of the path. No less intense was their hatred for all who varied from them within the fold of the same religion. Religion had thus become a broad avenue on which a man might walk haughtily, pouring out his hostility toward those of his own faith, destroying them by any means which came to hand, and giving God the glory for a man's progress in goodness.

BARRICADES

Instead of seeking to appease one's world, one may attempt to barricade himself against it. The threat to the self, which in fact is within the self, is understood to be without it and any one of many kinds of protection may be cast up to shield the self against the danger.

Self-concealment. Among the many kinds of self-concealment that are possible, attention is here drawn particularly to those forms of it which are expressed through speech. It is commonly said that language is a means of communication, and of course this is true; but the full import of the statement is not to be seen unless we also keep in mind that the purpose of the communication may be to divert or even to delude other persons. As has been observed by Harry Stack Sullivan,[11] a child learns to use language as a means of gaining security for himself. In order to attain that security, whether in childhood or afterward, one is often put in a situation where he feels compelled to use language as a way of shielding the self as he knows it to be from the view and comprehension of others. In this manner it comes about that language is often employed not truly as a means of communicating the self as it is, but as a means of shielding that self from the view of others.

When the self feels threatened and believes the threat to be from the outside, speech may be used for self-concealment in either of two extreme forms. One of these is to speak of oneself, if at all, only with great reserve, so that as little as possible of the self may be communicated, so that curious or hostile eyes may not peer within. What passes for great modesty may thus sometimes be due to a fear of damaging self-revelation.

The other extreme form in which speech may be employed as a means of self-concealment is volubility. The person who takes this method of screening himself is the "great talker," who pours out a torrent of words, beating down every comment from another, until, wearied with the attempt to share selves through conversation, his companions give him the verbal field to hold unchallenged. Over-activity in speech may thus serve to protect the self which actually is anxious concerning its own motives and status.

Self-encystment. Or, again, one who feels threatened may barricade himself in a sort of social cyst. He then becomes, as it were, a social capsule, resistant to the common adjustments and the usual give and take of ordinary life. The walls of the cyst in which one has immured himself may consist of some rigid pattern of living or of belief, or of some ritual, any of which may serve in some manner to protect the self against danger. The pattern or the ritual now becomes something to be cherished and preserved, otherwise its loss would arouse anxiety. The secondary anxiety which can be avoided becomes a substitute for a more primary anxiety whose nature cannot be faced. By devoting one's full energies to preserving the pattern intact, or to performing the ritual faithfully, one may stave off the potential secondary anxiety which would be aroused if the pattern were broken or the ritual not faithfully performed; and in such a way he can guard himself externally against some inward threat arising out of himself, whose true nature he either does not or cannot understand.

As we have already indicated, this self-encystment may take the form of becoming very rigid in social relations. It is a common historical phenomenon that when a social order is breaking up and another is taking its place, aristocrats become very insistent upon the punctilious observance of social customs which have descended from the old days. It has been a proverbial saying that an Englishman on duty in some jungle locality and fearful lest he should "go native" would dress for dinner every day. In short, by becoming a rigid devotee of some Emily Post, ancient or modern, one would protect himself against the social processes operative in one's surrounding world, with the changes of the self consequent upon participating in those processes.

Much the same purpose may be served by enclosing oneself within a rigid system of beliefs. Again it is a matter of common observation in religious history that in periods of far-reaching change which threaten to engulf an old order, many persons find security in the most determined effort to maintain unchanged a system of doctrine. It is not necessary to suppose that there is always a direct connection with a personal sense of guilt in such instances, but in some cases this appears unmistakably to be so. One of the most aggressive advocates of orthodoxy in religious doctrine in a certain city, for example, is homosexual. The tendency itself in this instance has proved unmanageable and seeks overt expression. The sense of guilt is perhaps intolerable, and apparently a solution has been found by a fierce insistence that in himself and in others there should be loyalty to a revered system of doctrine.

One of the most significant ways by which an individual who feels threatened may wall himself in, and thus protect himself, is by means of ritual. The existence of what is known as the compulsive ritual is familiar in psychiatric practice. There is, for example, a small family group in which the father is a very dominating character with a high moral code, and insistent upon strict obedience from his children, whom he seeks to control in virtually every detail of living. One of the children, a girl, has developed a ritual of performing a dance each night around a wooden pole. The rite is carried out with much secrecy and only became known by chance to the brother who, in turn, related it with much reluctance to a close friend of the family. Precisely what the role played by this ritual dance was in the life of this girl is not known; but apparently it had some function of guarding against or allaying the hostility which she felt toward the dominating father.

An almost interminable list of compulsive rituals could be brought together from the literature of psychiatric practice. It is rather generally held by psychiatrists that these rituals serve in some way to protect the self against its own sense of guilt.

The fact that self-made ritual often emerges spontaneously in persons having a deep sense of guilt, is of great significance to those who wish to grasp the nature of religious ritual, and especially the rites designed to placate the deity. For a number of decades it was the fashion to suggest that such rites were the product of priestcraft, imposed upon gullible folk for the priests' own private advantage. It now begins to appear at least equally probable that in their origin atonement rituals may have been spontaneously produced by the very persons themselves who were suffering from an overpowering sense of guilt.

It is possible that careful study of the factor of underlying hostility would throw further light on the origins of those Hebrew rituals intended to placate the deity. Two kinds of hostility in dynamic relationships are much in evidence in ancient Hebrew culture and in those other cultures with which the Hebrews had contact. We cannot avoid the possibility that the sense of guilt arising in connection with such hostility may have made atonement rituals an inward necessity. One of these was the hostility felt toward the king or other principal figure in the group. Modern research has brought to light some fascinating survivals of ancient customs which seem to give evidence of such hostility toward the king. Ritual enactment of the murder of the aged king appears to show or at least to suggest that in some cultures when the king had reached an advanced age he was ceremoniously put to death and then ceremoniously restored to life in the person of his son, his successor.

The second kind of hostility which must be taken into account is that between a father and his sons. Such hostility is much in evidence in the records of ancient Hebrew culture. It will be recalled, of course, that this culture was patriarchal, the father holding a position in which he exercised stern domination over his sons; a domination, moreover, in which one son by custom was frequently more highly favored than another. The hostility arising in these relationships deserves a much more frank consideration than it has yet received.

It is possible that the strength of hostility from father to child in this culture may be illustrated in the custom of passing a child through the fire. It must be said that the meaning of this expression is not altogether clear. Some students of the Old Testament believe it refers only to an ordeal, which might be cruel enough but not necessarily fatal. However, the light that has already been thrown upon the origin of other Hebrew rituals suggests the possibility that even if passing through the fire meant only an ordeal at the time these records were written, it may have been a survival of the actual sacrifice of children by fire. In any event the Hebrews seem to have been irresistibly drawn to the custom, and whatever the degree of cruelty represented by it, we can hardly deny its significance in parent-child relationships.

The hostility of sons toward the father lies with great frankness on the face of the Hebrew records themselves. It deeply colors the history of the patriarchs. It lies open at every turn in the story of David's sons. The steady demand that parents must be honored, and the stern penalties invoked against specific forms of disrespect, suggest how difficult it may have been to maintain the outward forms of respect in a patriarchal society when the very nature of that society itself did so much to breed hostility between parent and child. Such facts as these cannot be neglected in considering the nature and origins of Hebrew atonement ritual.

ALTERATION

The self, threatened by forces within but believing the danger to be outside, may develop another strategy quite different from that of appeasement or barricades. Lewis Carroll in his delightful fantasy *Alice in Wonderland* has it that Alice could change her size so as to meet the demands of the situation in which she was placed. Upon occasion she could shrink in size until she became so small as to escape unnoticed. On the other hand, however, she could become so large as to seize attention and command respect. The threatened self knows a strategy of this kind, which we may call the strategy of alteration, by means of which the self may be either contracted or expanded as a way of meeting the danger.

Self-contraction. One who is in peril because of internal forces which he cannot manage, and who believes the threat is outside himself, may take a role in which he becomes very small. It is as if he were saying, "See how insignificant I am! I could not possibly be of any danger to anyone!"

This is more than what is ordinarily called timidity. It is born of fear, but it is a fear which puts on quickly a small but very angelic stature. It is said, for example, that prisoners of war when brought in from territory where atrocities have been committed, frequently wear a most ingratiating smile, as if to say, "Just take one look at my face, and you will know I never did any of those things you are thinking about. It was somebody else."

What is known as slave mentality may be of this nature. Persons of the "master race" may be greatly deceived by the fawning attitude taken by the person whose position is that of slave. He seems anxious to please, ready to taste the dust at the feet of his master. To many who have spent much of life surrounded by Negro people, it has come as a shock to learn that beneath the obsequious attitude of the "white man's Negro" there may lie a carefully concealed but often symbolically expressed hatred whose strength could never have been guessed from any outward sign.

Self-expansion. The strategy of the threatened self in altering its size may be of an exactly opposite kind; in that event the motive is so to magnify the guilt that others, protecting, will rush to the rescue and disavow for him what he will not disavow for himself. Such a person reproaches himself in the hearing of others. He openly takes upon himself more than his fair share of blame. When some fault has been committed he brands himself as a monstrous sinner. If he can magnify his guilt to the point where his comrades will disavow it for him, it will then be they and not he saying, "Why, of all things! You are no such sinner as *that*!"

ATTACK

In the forms of guilt which we have been considering, the underlying hostility tends not to find overt expression but to be drained away into side channels of one sort or another. We have now to consider those outcroppings of guilt which have this common characteristic, that hostility finds some outlet in aggression, either against others or against one's own self. Here we have in view certain forms that may be taken to relieve anxiety by an attack upon other persons.

Self-justification. Among the many forms of self-justification of which human nature is capable there is one especially which deserves attention because of the strategy of counterattack that is employed. When the self is anxious over its own status, relief may be found by making another person, who represents the danger, still more anxious than oneself. It is as if we said, "Do you say my face is black? Well, get a mirror and look at your own!"

The story of Abner, in his relations with Ishbosheth the son of Saul, neatly illustrates this strategy. Abner had been an adherent of Saul's, and had taken his side in the conflict with David; but the time came when David's position in the nation was steadily becoming stronger while that of Saul was growing correspondingly weaker day by day. Abner's status was in jeopardy, to say nothing of his very head. Abner's record of dealings with the concubines of Saul was not a clean one, and as the fortunes of Saul's house declined, Ishbosheth, the heir, takes Abner to task. But the descendant of Saul had no more than got in a word of reprimand than Abner blazed forth at Ishbosheth with such a torrent of abuse as left the king's son cowering in fear, and unable to say more. By thus branding Ishbosheth as the true criminal, Abner could now turn his coat with a good conscience and go over to the side of David whom he had so lately opposed.

Children and adolescents often employ this method of reprisal, with great skill and effectiveness, in the relationships with their parents. For example, a child who has committed some misdeed may, by his bearing, so provoke the parent as to call out an especially severe punishment; then since the punishment is out of proportion to the misdeed, the parent is placed in the position of needing to seek forgiveness from the child, while the child, the original wrongdoer, is able to grant forgiveness to the parent.

Self-projection. When the endangering forces or impulses within oneself create anxiety which cannot be dealt with for what it is, one may project these impulses, or others akin to them, upon other persons, and then attack those persons. The ground for the attack as typically stated is some error, fault, or misdeed, which bears some kinship to an unacceptable element within the attacker himself.

The history of religion offers examples too numerous to mention. Much of the zeal manifested in religious persecutions appears to have motives of this general nature. The witch hunts in New England may be a case in point. In the late seventeenth century the sense of guilt was an active factor in New England experience. Especially does this seem to have been true in regard to sex morality. The code of sex morals was high, but from contemporary records as of church trials, we know that the actual conduct varied greatly from the professed code. In the Scripture, which played so great a part in New England thought, devotion to any other gods, or commerce with other spirits besides the Spirit of God, is often compared to unfaithfulness in the marriage relation. The psychological groundwork lay ready at hand for an attack upon those who had commerce with the spirits of evil. Belief in the existence and activity of just such spirits was a common possession.

In such an atmosphere Cotton Mather grew up. He had severe struggles of conscience, as his diary reveals, battling against some unnamed and unnamable temptation. Furthermore, the status of the church in New England was endangered, and by that much the status of its ministers was made the more uncertain, and hence became a cause of anxiety. Cotton Mather was a prime mover in the hunt for witches, and the people whom he so passionately fired to a white heat of zeal were ready enough to find evidences of witchcraft in their neighbors. Much that went to make up this strange passage in American history must remain obscure, and a subject for speculation; but it seems reasonable to suppose that no small part was played by an active sense of guilt projected upon others whose fault bore some kinship with moral flaws in highly placed clergy and laity; flaws which could not be faced for what they were.[12]

RETALIATION

The most obvious outlet for hostility is to strike back at the thwarting agent, getting an eye for an eye and a tooth for a tooth. But no society, whether it be as small as a family or as great as a nation, can allow the unregulated expression of the primitive impulse to destroy. As the expression of primitive hostility is regulated by the code and reinforced by the powerful emotional sanctions of family and religion, not only is primitive retaliation held in check so far as overt expression is concerned, but as we have seen, in some persons it cannot even be admitted to consciousness. Such an outcome is frequently regarded as a great moral victory, for we are sure to find some who will maintain that such a person has conquered hatred in himself and thus has subdued nature.

' It is well to understand what such an alleged victory means. Human nature is not so easily cheated as to give up to any pretender to authority, either its primitive impulses or its conscience. Neither of these can be denied without peril; and if no better solution for conflicts can be found, one will retaliate upon himself. In that event he will visit upon himself some punishment suited to the psychic crime which he has committed against himself.

Self-punishment. It is never to be supposed that all self-punishment is evil in the sense of being destructive of the self. By means of conscience, "superego," moral judgment, or call it what we will, one administers rebuke to himself, draws himself back from some abyss into which he might have tumbled, reins himself in against some outrage which he is fully capable of doing, and keeps himself, it may be, a more or less decent member of society. Without such sane self-speaking as belongs to a reasonable self-control, there could be no human society. It is well to say these things, for doctrines are abroad which would not only unleash the beast in man but keep it untamed and thus deny ourselves the possession of any world except one ruled by brute force which can have no end except to destroy itself. But conscience begins to pass beyond its creative function in proportion as it becomes a means or method by which one destructively punishes himself. For the time being we are chiefly concerned with the strange capacity of a man to do just that, for the human being is quite capable of injuring or even of destroying himself, for the reason that he has wished to, but would not, injure or destroy another whom he loves.

Instances of self-punishment are very numerous in clinical experience. Some psychiatrists, especially those of psychoanalytical persuasion, are inclined to equate the sense of guilt with self-punishment, and to regard self-punishment as the only true sign of guilt feelings. This is an extreme view, of a rather doctrinaire kind; the sense of guilt is too intricate to be tucked into one such pigeonhole. Nevertheless, the concept of self-punishment as it has been worked with in clinical experience offers a degree of explanation for much in human conduct which otherwise would seem wholly unaccountable. Let us turn to a few of the many possible examples.

Consider, for instance, the case of that person whose life is a long record of one failure after another. Anyone knows some person who, time after time, has been given every opportunity, but failed to utilize what others have done for him, and will carve out no niche for himself. The question of motives in such a case is always a perplexing one. Friends ask, "Why is it that he can't take hold?"

And he, the person most concerned, is least able to give any answer even to himself.

Probably no one would care to maintain that self-punishment is operative in all such cases, but in some it clearly is, when the motives are well understood. One such instance is that of a young man of good intelligence and good family, whose college career was a story of difficulty and failure in academic subjects, and moral escapades of a dubious character which kept him in constant hot water. He expressed both admiration and affection for his parents and could not understand why he himself was so great a trial to them. The father, a man of great determination and force of character, had influenced the son to choose law as a career. The father was paying the costs, and it seemed up to the son to make a record which would justify the father's confidence. But no such record was forthcoming.

As he began to arrive at a better understanding of himself, however, he faced within himself a hostility toward his father, long pushed back from open awareness, but of such great strength as to terrify him when he began to recognize it. His first reactions were ones of shame and horror at himself. But as he worked the matter through still further he came to see that his failures in college were serving a double purpose: one was to punish himself for the hostility which he felt toward the father, the other to punish the father by destroying the latter's dearest ambition, namely, that the son should succeed in the career of law which the father had chosen for him. He began to enter into a new and more honest relationship with his father, who fortunately responded eagerly to the new son emerging from the one who was. His college career, now his own and not another's, easily took care of itself.

Lampl[13] reports at some length the case of a man whose life was a story of failure—failure in love, failure in marriage, failure in business, failure in everything else, and one failure after another. The man was bewildered by himself, since he knew he had the capacity for success. During analysis the difficulty was finally traced to conflict with and hostility toward the father in very early life. Lampl gives the problem the interpretation peculiar to Freudians; but be that as it may, when the matter was faced out by recognizing the hostility and dealing squarely with it, the entire pattern of life was changed, and the man thereafter attained a fair measure of success both in his marriage and in his business affairs.

Or consider that category of curious human acts known by the name of purposeful accidents. It has been observed in clinical experience that not infrequently an individual who seems on the very verge of some coveted success meets with an accident which deprives him of its enjoyment. Was this his last fling of vengeance at himself, before he could seize the coveted prize? The aviator, far from home and over enemy territory, on his last flight before his leave is due, going down; the runner, slated for a race tomorrow with good prospects of victory, who is lamed the night before; the salesman who has all but landed a big contract, and then commits some absurd *faux pas*—these and many another event of their kind are often attributed to what we call overeagerness. Perhaps that is enough to explain most such unexpected outcomes, when success is just in reach. But in many cases where better knowledge of motives is possible, it has been found that an individual will often contrive to snatch from himself the very success which consciously he coveted most, and thereby visit some form of vengeance upon himself. Thus in a training school for delinquents a boy may be within a few days of winning that most coveted return to liberty, and then run away, with the result that he is again put in confinement and under discipline. Even more impressive still is the record of many criminals who contrive as with an infallible instinct to commit some crime for which they will be apprehended and punished.

Still again, in cases of maternal rejection unconscious motives of self-punishment often appear to be present in both mother and child. We have already had occasion to see how, in many instances of this kind, mother and child are bound together by ties of hatred which neither is capable of breaking. As if to atone for her own hostility, the mother may become oversolicitous for the child's welfare, while the child, as if also to atone for his hatred, will sometimes take a sort of servant's role in the household.

For example, there is the W family. Mrs. W came to the clinic asking help with her son, Jack. Jack, a large, overgrown boy of fifteen, had been taking money, first small sums, and then larger ones. Mrs. W expressed a great affection for Jack, and as an evidence of his feeling toward her of a similar kind she related that he still sat on her lap with his arms about her every evening. More than that, she said, he was so helpful around the house, sewing, cooking, washing, and in general assisting her with the household work. He seemed to care nothing for getting out and getting a job, but preferred to stay at home and help his mother.

It required many hours of conversation to enable the mother to say openly that she had not wanted this child before he was born, because her husband was out of work and she herself was ill. But after he was born, she was ashamed of her feelings toward him and had showered him with attention. He had not been a strong child and she had nursed him with unusual care. She had kept him close to her, and shielded him from hard knocks, and he had become her shadow. Now that the boy had reached the age of fifteen, the tension was becoming unbearable to both, yet neither could break it, and meanwhile they were tied together, the one by her over-solicitude, and the other by his overhelpfulness, each atoning by this spurious "love" for a hatred which he could not admit.

Once more, illness may be a form of self-punishment. The range of illnesses in which unconscious motives of self-punishment may have a part is large. And only a physician is competent to speak in this complex area. Within the last two or three decades psychiatrists have done a vast amount of work with the so-called neurotic illnesses, that is, with forms of illness for which there is no ascertainable physical basis, or at least none sufficient to account for the complaints. In these, as we have just said, the disguised motive of self-punishment often is a highly significant element. Among numerous possible examples, one must suffice.

Rose S, twenty-four years of age and the mother of three children, had begun to suffer from severe headaches. One day while bathing the youngest child in a tub she became dizzy, and lost consciousness temporarily, but she was able to attract a neighbor's attention and was helped to her bed where she lost consciousness completely, awakening to find a physician attending her. This was the beginning of a long illness and a correspondingly long course of treatment during which no physical basis for her complaint could be found.

Investigation disclosed that in her earlier married life she had been happy, but near the time of the birth of the last child she discovered that her husband had gambled away a substantial sum of money which the two together had saved. Promises of reform were not kept, and the gambling continued. Her happiness turned to ashes. She made it known to the physician that the youngest child did not hold the same place in her affections as the others, but she was extremely reticent upon the subject and declined to discuss it fully, resenting any implications that her attitude toward this child was anything other than that of a normal mother. The physician, however, believed that the child had become to the mother a symbol of her marital unhappiness, an unhappiness so deep that unconsciously she wished to destroy the child, the impulse to that end being so strong that day when the child was in the tub as to horrify the mother and precipitate the illness. The physician regarded this interpretation as the more probable because the mother frequently intimated that she had some deep secret which she would never disclose, not even if disclosing it would enable her to get well. Indeed, she seemed to find a sort of peace through her illness, and the physician understood this to mean that by the illness she was daily punishing herself for impulses which she could neither avow and be rid of, nor express and thereby become still more horribly guilty.[14]

Self-destruction. The self, confronting impulses which it can neither admit, express, nor control, has another recourse even more drastic than that of continuing self-punishment, and that is self-destruction. How large a proportion of suicide is attributable to conflicts of this nature which the individual finds completely insoluble, it would be unwise even to guess. By the very nature of the cases the final moment of utter bafflement which leaves the individual with no other apparent recourse than to end his life, must remain an almost completely unknown land. Notes and other documents left by persons who have chosen this bleak road are suggestive but by no means conclusive, since even in death the tortured self may still seek to hide its deepest motives and guard itself to the very end with a pathetic robe of decency.

But aside from those who physically destroy themselves by one sudden act, there is a large group of persons whom Menninger[15] calls by the suggestive name of chronic suicides. These are persons who carry self-punishment to such an extreme that they begin to destroy themselves, but do it slowly, bit by bit, day by day. This may be done, suggests Menninger, by many means, such as alcoholism, many kinds of neurotic illness, need for repeated surgical operations, and perhaps by the development of certain conditions which have ordinarily been regarded as "physical" in nature, such as arteriosclerosis.

Menninger's views are regarded by many physicians as quite extreme, and only a physican is competent to deal in detail with the material which Menninger presents. For our purposes the principal interest lies in the fact that many medical men, thoroughly trained as they are in the methods of modern scientific medicine, should be seriously disposed to widen the range of human ailments due chiefly to emotional conflicts; and that any modern medical man at all should give us a picture of the destructive results of a sense of guilt far more graphic, because more realistic, than any hell imagined by the poets. The modern physician apparently understands better than the modern theologian that there is such a thing as continuing destruction in human bodies where the worm will not die and the fire will not be quenched.

DISINTEGRATION

There remains yet another large group of conditions, the psychoses, in some of which the sense of guilt often figures prominently.

The psychoses are the so-called mental diseases, the insanities. In a vivid figure of speech Carl Whitaker has compared the neuroses and the psychoses to two different conditions of a camel. In the neuroses some last straw has nearly broken the camel's back, but by re-sorting the straws, the camel is able to get up and go on. In the psychoses the camel's back is broken; he is down, and he cannot get up. Again, in common speech we often say of such a person that he has gone completely to pieces, a comparison which at least has the value of suggesting that in some of the psychoses the self has been broken up into two or more selves with the result that the person cannot present a united and consistent front to the world.

The sense of guilt in the psychoses would, itself, be a fit subject for a treatise whose worth might be almost immeasurable, but one which at present perhaps no person is capable of preparing adequately. For our part we shall attempt no more than to point to a few aspects of the matter, and then more by way of question than by way of answers.

Dissociation of Personality. We begin with a condition not properly included under psychoses, but of great interest in this connection because it represents in an extreme form the solution of a moral problem by frankly splitting into two or more personalities. The condition is variously known as dual personality, multiple personality, or dissociated personality. The literature of psychology and medicine contains a relatively small number of cases of this kind.

One of the most recent of these is a case called Sara K, studied with great care by Lipton.[16] Sara, a young married woman, was found wandering aimlessly on the street, unable to recall her own identity or to give any clear account of herself. Taken to a hospital, she received medical care extending over many months.

In the hospital it began to be observed that Sara's behavior was not uniform. At times she was quiet, moody, reserved, and complained of many pains. At other times, she was cheerful, gay, even boisterous; and relatively insensible to pain. Then it was observed that she passed suddenly from one to the other of these states, and it was recognized that Sara had become two personalities. There was no true continuity between the two, and she was given two names to distinguish the two personalities, Sara being the quiet one, often depressed and suffering; while Maude was the name given to the other personality, which was sensuous, bright, and carefree.

Only gradually did the story come out, much of it then under hypnosis. Sara was a daughter of a father who was not very intelligent but was very domineering, and of a mother who was rigid in all her attitudes. Sara had little affection for either parent, but was ardently devoted to Godfrey, her brother. At an early age she had begun an incestuous relation with him which was continued with some intermissions for many years. Her father had forced her into incestuous relations. Those with the father she loathed and detested, but to Godfrey she was passionately devoted. Beyond this, there had also been promiscuity outside the family. Marriage, although happy in some respects, had done little to solve the fundamental issues for Sara. The record disclosed that long before the frank split in personality she had undergone milder swings.

During the time in the hospital, as Sara she was a woman of sensitive conscience, burdened with guilt, dejected, apprehensive, and complaining of physical pain. But, it was observed, when the sense of guilt became too great for her to bear, she passed suddenly into the personality of Maude; and Maude had no conscience at all. She talked freely then of Godfrey and of her relation with him, had no shame, and was ready to abandon herself completely to her strong primitive impulses. As Sara she could remember nothing of what she said, thought, or did when she was Maude; while as Maude she was equally unable to recall any part of her life when she was Sara. In such a manner this young woman, baffled by her own acute moral problem, solved it by becoming two personalities within the one body. As the one she was tormented with guilt feelings. As the other she was free. But on such a basis normal life was impossible, for her actions were incalculable, and she was a source of danger both to herself and to others. If therapy is not successful there seems to be no future except continuing hospitalization, possibly with schizophrenia and deterioration ahead.

Psychotics. In the psychotic condition known as schizophrenia, and in some of the severely depressed states, the sense of guilt often is very prominent. One may feel oppressed by guilt so tremendous as to be overwhelming, crushing. Many of these persons are obsessed with the thought of the "unpardonable sin," which they seldom can name, but because of which they suffer. Many have hallucinations of sight or sound, in which they see, perhaps, monstrous shapes threatening them, or hear voices charging them with sinful acts.

Some of the psychotic conditions which have no known physical cause are conditions in which a sense of guilt is most evident, although the presence of a sense of guilt may occur with brain tumor, arteriosclerosis, etc., and is by no means restricted to psychoses without known physical basis. As long as the causes remain unknown and therefore an object for speculation, as is to be expected, medical men are not of one mind as to the reasons. There is the group who remain convinced that could we but discover them, there are physical causes and physical reasons for each psychotic condition. Possibly, it is urged, many persons are born into life with a physical constitution which renders such an outcome inevitable. On the other hand there are those who are equally convinced that at least many of the so-called functional psychoses are the result of some kind of inadequate living in human relationships.

As soon as medical science can speak with finality upon so momentous a question and prove its case beyond doubt, that verdict must be accepted and lived with. But as long as there remains any reasonable ground for believing that even one form of "insanity" grows out of malignant human relationships, just so long must we seriously regard the sense of guilt as possibly being a factor contributing to that dreadful scourge which strikes both the humble and the great.

Since knowledge in this area is still so fragmentary, especial interest attaches to the studies of Boisen in what might be called the moral problems involved in schizophrenia. Under the general term "schizophrenia" are grouped a number of conditions which are by no means alike. Boisen found that among the cases he studied the various types did not show a uniform percentage of improvement and return to ordinary life. His attention was especially caught by the fact that schizophrenics who had episodes of panic showed a better percentage of recovery than was the case with the drifters. Upon studying the case histories carefully, and on the basis of his own knowledge of the persons concerned, Boisen came to the conclusion that these two types of reaction in schizophrenics represented two different patterns of response to some crucial moral problem which had been faced in living. The panic type fought back when they faced their moral Rubicon, and a good proportion of them got well. The drifter type, on the other hand, surrendered in the face of a moral issue, gave up the fight, and drifted into a condition where all moral standards were down, with the primitive impulses of unchecked nature standing out naked; few of these persons recovered. From such material Boisen has come to think of some form of mental illness as being comparable to fever in the body, and he speaks of these as nature's effort to heal, that is, as it were, to get rid of a moral infection which is sure to injure and may even destroy the self unless it is fought.[17]

Retrospect

We have now reached the point of turning from questions of conflict and guilt to those which concern redemption and the means by which it may be brought about. It will be well, therefore, to look at the salient features of the landscape which has been traversed. If the statements about to be made seem to be dogmatic it is only because they are put compactly for the sake of brevity.

The sense of guilt arises out of malignant human relationships. It is associated with anxiety and hostility. Guilt, anxiety, and hostility are so bound together, and each breeds so much more of its own kind, that often there is great difficulty in knowing where the primary problem lies, so that a man and his associates are often honestly deluded as to the nature of the fundamental underlying moral issue. The sense of guilt is so painful that ordinarily the self wishes nothing so much as to cover its true character from every eye, whether of the neighbor, the family, or one's own self.

Since the sense of guilt arises out of malignant human relationships and since these relationships began when the individual himself was helpless, there is a large measure of justice in the contention both of ancient and of modern times that the responsibility for our plight lies outside ourselves. But in every relationship one responds as truly as he is acted upon; and if he is locked in guilt from which he cannot escape, he is in that position because his hostility is his own. To disavow his own responsibility and thus to seek release is partly just, but wholly ineffective, since his anxiety, his hostility, and his guilt still remain, in spite of his protestations, to torment him and perhaps to destroy him. He must therefore look beyond himself for release, not because his guilt belongs to any other than himself, but because as long as he stands alone he can find no way to be released.

✄ V ✄

THE DESCENT INTO HELL

WHEN WE BEGIN to ask how release from guilt may be had, there are certain points which cannot be too strongly emphasized if the heart of the issue is to be kept in view.

The first of these is that anxiety and hostility are more basic than the sense of guilt. The sense of guilt, whether in its conscious or unconscious form, may be compared to a barometer of which two things have to be said. The conditions of the elements which the barometer is reporting are more important than the barometer itself; and, as it happens in this case, the barometer cannot be depended upon to give an unfailingly accurate report.

Therefore, as a second point of emphasis, a thorough alteration of the sense of guilt can be made only in proportion as its underlying causes are altered. Self-evident as this is, perhaps it is as often honored in the breach as in the observance of it. Both in religion and in medical practice it is far easier to tinker with the surface symptoms or outcroppings of guilt than it is to deal radically and profoundly with the malignant factors which are causing them. This "tinkering" can be done either by decreasing or by increasing the sense of guilt without getting at fundamental causes. Both religion and psychiatry propose that release from guilt may be had. Neither of the two makes any offer to govern itself by what the other does. Religion, when it knows itself, is no imitator of psychiatry. On the other hand, psychiatry holds no brief for religion. Yet both are concerned with the healing of men, and in practice it is becoming increasingly evident that each knows resources which profoundly illumine the work of the other.

Accordingly, as we approach first the concept and practice of therapy as known in the clinic, and then redemption as known in religion, especially in Christianity, we shall be seeking points of kinship where each throws light upon the other; and we shall seek constantly to hold in view the point already urged, namely, that anxiety and hostility are more basic than the sense of guilt itself.

PRISONERS OF HOSTILITY

Man has made himself the prisoner of his own hostility. If one doubts it, let him try the experiment of dividing contemporary mankind into two classes, the one consisting of all those persons who are imprisoned in some manner by hostility and its results; the other, containing those who are free from it in every respect. Could he find any to put in the second class except a little handful of people who live on the outskirts of the earth and have not yet tasted the fruits of western "progress"?

The first class would contain an innumerable company, but the prisons which contain them are different. If war is thought of as the overt expression of hostility between nations, it is relevant to remember that in the United States alone during 1945 approximately one citizen out of each twelve was under arms, in uniform, having suspended all normal living and having made himself available to become an agent for the destruction of life and property among the enemy. The structures which we literally call by the name of prisons, house continually a substantial percentage of the population who are undergoing confinement and punishment because of hostile acts toward their fellow citizens. Hospitals of all descriptions contain another not inconsiderable proportion of the population who are incapacitated because of hostile acts directed against them, or because of their own hostility turned in some manner upon themselves. If we add all engaged in caring for these sick and imprisoned persons, and all those directly engaged in producing the sinews of war, it might not be an unreasonable guess to suppose that one person out of every five within that year in the United States was more or less directly imprisoned by hostility.

But from what we might call indirect imprisonment who among us is free in *any* year? The financial costs of war, courts, prisons, police, hospitals, clinics, correctional institutions, and the like, must be provided through taxation, and these taxes spare no man's purse. But there are still less tangible forms of bondage to hostility which evade all calculations. What with refugeeism, "cold wars," purges, resentment over military service, and above all the cold fear of extinction by ever more lethal bombs, our world is drenched in suffering so great as almost to anesthetize us against anguish which otherwise would be unbearable.

Since the prison which our hostility has woven around us defies imagination when it is regarded on the larger scale, it is better to pick up again the situation of individuals who, as microcosms, make up the universe of suffering due to hostility. This might be done in the greatest variety of ways, but we must here be content with presenting the matter in the form of a dilemma which a man faces when his own hostility is not dealt with at its roots.

In an article having great suggestive as well as direct value, Spafford Ackerly has shown that delinquent behavior may be thought of as a sort of alternative to neurosis in the lives of youths who have been emotionally thwarted in their dynamic relationships.[1] In the cases studied deep hostility has been aroused in these youths who have been so thwarted. If the hostility thus aroused found no open expression, the youths tended to become neurotic and thus to a degree incapacitated for normal living. On the other hand, if they could express the hostility they tended to avoid neurosis, but they then tended to come into conflict with society through forms of behavior known as delinquency. Thus while neurosis had been avoided, the problem of hostility remained to be dealt with.

The chains forged for themselves by two persons in a dynamic relationship have already been referred to in previous connections, but the situation can hardly be too often brought to view, for in it is to be found a world war reduced to a domestic scale and lived out, perhaps, between husband and wife or parent and child.

Take for example the situation which has developed in the G family. Mrs. G came to the clinic very tearful, saying that her son Howard was too much for her and her husband and she requested help. As for the dynamics of the relationship between the mother and the son, it became evident eventually that the boy had been rejected emotionally by the mother before he was born; but our interest here lies in seeing what the relationship had become by the time Howard was nearing twenty years of age.

Howard was a strong and husky young man who had been rejected by the Selective Service because of diabetes. Kept thus at home, he yet was physically able to work and earned good pay when he did work, but most of the time he refused all employment, remaining in the house, demanding money of his parents, and constantly reminding them that it was their duty to support him until he was twenty-one.

The mother's resentment was both deep and open; "Of course you cannot love a son like this," she would say, and yet she was not capable of standing up to him and refusing his demands. An older brother sent home $75.00 a month to be put in savings, but Howard demanded the money, threatened to burn the safety box if it were not turned over to him, and the mother yielded to him, afraid even to call the police, with the result that the older brother's savings had been spent without his knowledge.

Meanwhile relations within the family were in a state of open warfare. Howard addressed his father as "my drunkard dad," referred to his mother as "my lunatic mom," and when she crossed him he had been known to drench her with a pan of cold water.

This is their prison, in which two persons, mother and son, have shackled themselves together by bonds of hostility, anxiety, and guilt which neither can break. Precisely here lies the role of the therapist. A person has come to the point where the self is undergoing destruction, but a destruction from which he cannot extricate himself. How, then, can the therapist be of aid to him?

THERAPY

Therapy, of course, is not restricted to those persons who are given the name of therapists. In homes of every description, behind counters, desks, and benches, probably in most communities and certainly in all occupations, are to be found persons who exercise the healing art over the souls of men. In no way have they been especially trained for the part. They are "naturals" for it, as we say. Often they themselves do not know how they do it; they only *do* it, and are glad they can. To them, persons in trouble go as to a magnet, and come away stronger. It was said of Phillips Brooks that when he passed along the crooked streets of old Boston, those who beheld him took a deeper breath and were refreshed. It was said of Peter, not unreasonably, that even his shadow cast upon the sick brought health.

These things need to be said, and never wholly lost to view, because just as the soul of man is an intricate place, so is its therapy an equally intricate process. Too great a simplification in regard to the one is as serious an error as it is in regard to the other.

Nevertheless, if therapy is to be a science as well as an art, the nature of what takes place must be grasped if it is to be reproduced by other persons or by the same persons under different conditions.

During the twentieth century a vast amount of work by skilled persons has gone into the attempt to make therapy a science. There are crosscurrents in the thought concerning, and divergencies in the practice of, therapy which can be appreciated in their fullness only by a physician who has devoted years to this work. It is said that the tendency to develop schools of thought and of practice sharply distinguished from one another has been much greater in Europe than in the United States, and that in the latter country the tendency generally is in the direction of eclecticism; that is, a readiness to use those concepts and methods which "work."

For such reasons it seems wise, for the purposes of these lectures, to point out certain factors which appear in therapy, rather than attempting an inclusive description of psychotherapy, for the latter could be successfully done only by a physician.

Furthermore, it will be obvious to those with thorough knowledge of psychotherapy that we select certain factors which have an especial significance for religion. There are many procedures in therapy which are wholly in place there, and are of much interest to a psychiatrist, but which have only a remote significance, if any, as illustrating meanings in religion.

We shall now present a case, and afterward turn to the consideration of some of the factors in therapy. The case to be reported involves, among other things, hostility between mother and son; and it will be noted that two therapists appear, one a physician in relation with the son; the other a psychiatric social worker in relation with the mother. This relatively new method is now frequently employed in clinics, but the salient point is not the fact that two persons appear in the role of therapist, so much as it is the role which the therapist takes in the relationship. Furthermore, as the sense of guilt is uppermost in our inquiry, attention is especially given here to the relationship with the mother since in her case the sense of guilt was more obvious.

THE OSBORNES

Mr. and Mrs. Osborne came into the clinic together. Mr. Osborne is a garage owner. Mrs. Osborne is a warm, intelligent person. There are five children and she spoke of them, including Mike, with expressions of affection. Mike is the youngest. All the children have made good adjustments, and get along well with other children, except Mike, age about ten, who is brilliant but was doing poor school work, daydreaming, and was stealing. The sums stolen have been growing larger, the last time being about eight dollars. He had run away from home, and the police had had to get him.

In the first interview Mrs. Osborne evidently was seeking a way to account for Mike's behavior. She went at the matter indirectly, saying that she had asked her sister if she could think of any reason. The sister had replied that perhaps it went back to the time when Mike was a year old and had to be in the hospital with an infected foot. In telling this story the mother became so emotional that she had to stop talking. She was asked what this had meant to her. Her reply indicated that it was pity for herself rather than pity for the boy. She said all the children had been sick at one time, that she herself was sick and in the hospital with pneumonia. After she left the hospital she had no help and had to have the care of all the children when she herself should have had someone to nurse her. This was the first indication that she felt anything except warmth toward this boy.

In the second interview she showed more confidence in the worker and was able to release more of her hostility toward Mike. She did this partly by comparing Mike with another son. She described the oldest boy, James, in glowing terms, making comparison between the two boys always in favor of James. She said Mike would ask her, "Why do you always laugh at James' jokes and not at mine?" She said she replied, "I listen to your jokes a thousand times and they aren't funny anyway." Then she spoke of all the friends Mike had made since living in the city, saying that every one of them was peculiar in some way. By contrast she described the friends of her other children, saying that they all were nice persons.

In the third interview the hostility came out still more openly, due to the fact that Mike had just stolen money from his brother, and again the mother's preference for James was expressed more clearly. She showed high regard for everything that James said or thought. She said the minister told them they must not punish Mike too severely; Mike, said the minister, was a borderline case and if they punished him too severely they might push him over the border. When Mrs. Osborne reported this advice at home, James had felt outraged. "No wonder Mike steals," protested James, "when he never gets punished for it, and only has to pay the money back."

Then Mrs. Osborne raised the same question with the worker: What do you think? Should we punish him for stealing, or not? The question was turned back to her. The worker asked what would have happened if the boys had settled their differences between them—if James had taken the responsibility of settling his difficulties with Mike himself. Mrs. Osborne stated she had told James to do just that, but James had answered, "Why, you couldn't punish a little kid like that! When you look at those weak, puny little hands you just don't have the courage to do anything to him!"

In describing this conversation with James, Mrs. Osborne herself displayed hostility in a dramatized form, stretching out her own hands and shaking them to illustrate James' words, her face and voice meanwhile expressing contempt and loathing for the "weak, puny little hands."

In the next interview Mrs. Osborne reported that Mike was worse than ever. He had stolen three times in one week, one of those times being from a person visiting in the home. The worker had tried to bring out the fact that parents have a right to feel differently about their children. It was difficult, she said, to love every one of them in precisely the same way. She was trying to help Mrs. Osborne handle the guilt she was feeling because of her own relationship with the son. Mrs. Osborne immediately assented, describing why she liked each one of the children for a special reason, including Mike in the description. She said Mike had always had more attention than the other children because he had demanded more attention.

The question was then taken up, What does Mike want out of life that he is not getting? Mrs. Osborne, in reply, again asserted that she recognized she did not feel the same toward Mike as toward her other children.

It probably is significant that the interview for the following week was broken on the ground of Mike's being ill. Evidently Mrs. Osborne welcomed the interruption of the interviews, for it appeared that during this interval she herself was struggling with the more clearly emerging sense of guilt within herself.

In the next interview both Mr. and Mrs. Osborne came, and they reported that Mike was definitely improving. They said he no longer had that furtive look in his eyes. Behind this opening statement lay something still more important. They had discussed with Mike how he might pay back the sums he had stolen. Mrs. Osborne said, "It must seem a hopeless thing to him because he has so little to pay it with, and he would have to stay in debt always." Between themselves they had discussed cancelling the debt, but she and her husband had agreed that this would not be best. They had told Mike that his father would have to punish him if he continued to steal, but Mike had said, "He won't have to. I'm through stealing." To that the mother had replied, "Mike, we are going to increase your allowance from twenty-five cents to thirty-five cents so that you can begin to pay back what you have taken and still have something left over for a show, carfare, ice cream, or candy."

It was plain that this incident marked a turning point in the relationships between Mike and his mother and father. Mrs. Osborne described how much it had meant to Mike to have his allowance increased, and in giving the description she manifested a kind of feeling different from that which she had previously displayed toward him. Evidently the increase in the allowance, small though it was, symbolized an increase in the genuine affection which Mike had needed.

Mrs. Osborne described other incidents at home in which she and Mike had shared in little things, such as the search for a lost football; and she responded readily to the question whether there might be still other things she and Mike might do together, such as planning an afternoon in town when both might go.

Meanwhile the physician's interviews with Mike, which we have not here reported, had been proceeding. On the same day as the interview with the mother last mentioned, Mike had said, "Sometimes you feel just like you want to kill somebody, and then you get over it." As he spoke he picked up a doll which, in Mike's play, had been a killer, and turned the doll into a dancer springing from place to place with a light heart.

In its very nature, play therapy is symbolic; thus it is easy for a child to use symbolism as a way of expressing feelings which are too painful to put into words. Again, he may resort to symbolism in letting the therapist know he feels strong enough to break the relationship and be "on his own." In the next interview with Mike, out of a clear sky the boy said, "My snowball is getting bigger." The physician asked, "I wonder how big the snowball is now?" Mike answered, "Almost big enough." The physician inquired, "How much longer will it take?" To which Mike immediately replied, "About two weeks."

The boy had made one other cryptic statement in the same interview, saying, "You know, it's wrong to say a guy is out of his mind. You should say, the mind is out of the guy."

In the remaining two interviews the case was brought to a close. Mrs. Osborne again described Mike's progress with much pride, and as far as the clinic is concerned, they left to carry on in the new relationship they had achieved. The story is not over, for no such story ends, but we must leave it here.

FACTORS IN THERAPY

Certain factors in therapy are now to be examined more closely. It is suggested that these are present in any truly therapeutic process, whatever the conception of the basic nature of therapy. As we have previously observed, the conceptions of the nature of therapy are not uniform for all schools of therapy, and we are not attempting a description of *all* that therapy means in *any* school of therapy. Instead—to repeat—*we are pointing to certain factors in psychotherapy which have an especial significance for the understanding of the Christian religion and the deeper appreciation of its resources by pastor and people.*

As for cases to illustrate the operation of the various factors to be named, no one actual case can be expected to bring out fully all the factors which are involved, but the case just cited may be considered a background against which many of these factors will stand out more plainly.

A preliminary remark regarding terminology must be made. We need two simple but very inclusive terms to indicate, on the one hand, the person in need of help, and on the other hand, the person giving it. No one term for either purpose is entirely satisfactory. As for the first, we need a term to connote an element in experience common to the patient, the client, the parishioner, the delinquent, and the criminal. For that purpose we shall here use the term "the sufferer," intending by that word to keep before ourselves one element which is common to them all. As for the second, we need one term to connote a function common to the psychiatrist, the social worker, the minister, and any others who may take on that function in human relationships. For that purpose we shall use here the term "the therapist," which only means "the healer." By this means we shall hope to keep before ourselves a career of dedication to which many have devoted themselves, whether they think primarily of the cure of the body or the cure of the soul.

Establishing a Relationship

When the sufferer comes to the therapist the first and most obvious fact is that the sufferer needs help. Seldom, however, does he tell the therapist at the outset the kind of help he most desires to receive. He may have been sent or brought to the therapist by other persons, more or less against his own will; in that event much time is required to establish an honest and frank relationship between sufferer and therapist. This is extremely difficult to achieve if the sufferer has any grounds for believing that the therapist is in league with any person or any group attempting to reform him or to use him for their own ends. Such a sufferer can successfully defy any individual on earth to enter unbidden into his own inner castle. He requires reassurance to the effect that *he* is the person who counts in the relationship between sufferer and therapist, and that the therapist has not the remotest interest in "pushing him around" for the sake of the parents, or the school, or the court, or the relatives, or anyone else. That reassurance when given in words will be vain unless the relationship itself quickly proves the claim to be a fact.

Again, the sufferer may have come entirely of his own accord. If so, by that fact he has symbolically stated very eloquently, "I need you." In that event, or if he first came unwillingly and then eventually thawed into rapport, the way begins to open for him to let the therapist know what he desires. The sufferer is likely to do this only with great caution and reserve in the earlier part of the relationship. Very commonly he begins by talking of some matter which is not truly his chief concern. By this means he tests out the therapist, and if he is disappointed in the results, he can withdraw from the relationship without having dangerously exposed the deeper needs.

RE-LIVING

In proportion as he comes to trust the therapist he begins to lay open the place where the hurt is most grievous. This may happen slowly throughout a number of interviews, or it may come tumbling out in a rush of words which sometimes overwhelm the sufferer himself. This is the point or the factor in therapy which we have tried to designate by the term "re-living," for here the sufferer lives over again that part of his experience which has baffled him and defeated him.

There is never a way of knowing in advance what will be brought out in this re-living of an experience which to the sufferer is distressing in the extreme. There is little value, if any, in rehearsing here the possibilities. The therapist goes by no book or chart. If he is truly a therapist he receives precisely what this sufferer brings out to the light. In doing that he does something else also at the same time: in the words of one psychiatrist, he goes down into this person's own little private hell with him.

In bringing up to light and re-living a disturbing emotional experience or problem, such profound results follow as to lead some to attribute the principal value to the sufferer's acts, and thus to lose sight of the possibility that the acts gain their value chiefly from the fact that they themselves have taken place in the sufferer's relationship with the therapist.

For example, high value is often given to what is called emotional catharsis, in which the sufferer, as it were, empties out or disgorges from himself the hostility, the guilt, or whatever else of a damaging emotional sort he may have held within himself too long. It requires but a little reflection to remind one that the meaning and value of any profound "catharsis" of emotional material must depend upon the person to whom it is made as well as the act itself.

It probably is wise to regard confession also in the same way. Doubtless there is one aspect of what we commonly call confession which has value to the person himself apart from the individual who hears it; rather, it would be truer to say that one sometimes confesses openly in order that all who will may hear it, for such a man wishes now to set himself right once and for all before all men in regard to some matter where hitherto he has concealed and

equivocated until he can bear it no longer. This aspect of confession has been symbolized among many people and in many ages
by public acts which signify that the guilty person is openly
expelling from himself some evil thing such as a foul spirit, a
devil, and the like.

But there is confession sometimes, perhaps often, to be made
which derives its value not only from the fact that a sufferer makes
it, but also from the fact that he makes it to one greater and
stronger than himself, and in so doing gives up the hopeless
attempt any longer to carry what he himself is not great enough
to sustain. Carl G. Jung pointed to this meaning of confession when
he wrote, "It seems to be a sin in the eyes of nature to hide our
insufficiency just as much as to live entirely on our inferior side.
There appears to be a conscience in mankind which severely
punishes the man who does not somehow and sometime, at whatever cost to his pride, cease to defend and assert himself, and
instead confess himself fallible and human. Here we find a key to
the great significance of true, unstereotyped confession—a significance known in all the initiation and mystery cults of the ancient
world, as is shown by a saying from the Greek mysteries, 'Give
up what thou hast, and then thou wilt receive.' "[2]

Much interest attaches to a form of re-living, which could be
called confession, made in the presence of a group and not in the
presence of one individual only. There is a long history of public
confession in the presence of religious groups, a story which it
would be out of place to recount here, except to say that sooner
or later it seems always to have brought dangerous repercussions
and even disaster. There is, however, another form of public
"re-living" of deep emotional experiences which has recently been
employed with psychological rather than distinctly religious motives.
There is, for example, the recent "psycho-drama," used with

persons from the armed forces who have broken under the strains of warfare and wartime conditions. Here the sufferer goes upon a stage and in the presence of other sufferers more or less like himself, acts out the problem or the conflict from which he suffers. Thus far the method must be considered as still experimental, but it has received considerable approval. It remains to be seen whether the method will eventually produce an undesirable back-wash comparable to that found so often in consequence of public religious confession.

However, there seem to be some significant differences between the two. In the psycho-drama the sufferer enacts a problem in the presence of others who are passing through an experience very like his own and who, presumably, can enter into it with him as comrades. But the action is in the third person and may enact the sufferer's own conflict only vaguely or not at all, yet all in conflict seem to benefit as they participate in the process of the drama. In the case of public religious confession it seems commonly to have been true that the group who heard the confession regarded themselves as the righteous sitting in judgment upon the sinner, and the experience of the one confessing has often been an excruciating agony against which hardier souls would rebel and under which tenderer ones would break with shame.

Acceptance

As the sufferer's conflict is being re-lived in his relationship with the therapist, something new in the sufferer's emotional career is taking place: he is being accepted exactly as he is by the person to whom he turns for help. We have already said that he brings out the most painful material cautiously; commonly he fills up the relationship with less important things until he has discovered step by step how the therapist responds to him as a person. In proportion as he gains confidence in the therapist he is able to bring out the deeper and more painful feelings. This was illustrated, for example, in the case of Mrs. Osborne. The frank preference for James rather than Mike could not be admitted at first. The same was true in regard to the hostility toward Mike; in the first stage of the relationship she spoke of Mike with warmth, but there came an hour when she shook with her rage as she dramatized her own feelings toward his "weak, puny little hands."

One crucial test of the therapist is his ability to accept this person as the latter's deeper emotions are being re-lived. Can he continue unmistakably to be emotionally on the sufferer's side as this "private hell" is entered to its very bottom? The therapist may use words of reassurance such as saying that every person has a right to his own feelings, but the reassurance is only a verbal means to a more important emotional end. The total bearing of the therapist demonstrates whether the words themselves are true or false.

It may not be forgotten, then, that the therapist himself is "on trial" during every instance of the therapeutic relationship. Only by most genuinely accepting the sufferer as things now stand, is there ground for legitimate hope that the sufferer can emerge into being what, as yet, he is not.

To the person who attempts therapy from distinctively religious motives, acceptance presents problems to him personally of which he may be only dimly aware. Because of his own training he is likely to have in mind a moral and spiritual goal which he wishes the sufferer to reach. Commonly he supposes that he can achieve this by telling the sufferer what to do. Not infrequently he nimbly by-passes the hell in human experience which is before him by giving the sufferer phrases from Scripture and from theology describing his condition, and thus he verbally eludes the very reality of the damnation which he is attempting to describe to the person who is in the midst of it. Such a man does not even hear the sufferer, but rushes upon him with words, overwhelms him, leaves him in his unillumined suffering, much as the good priest of Jerusalem left the stricken traveler by the wayside. This is not merely a matter of being morally outraged because of the feelings and acts of the sufferer; of that danger in pastoral therapy much has already been said elsewhere. Rather, this is non-acceptance of the sufferer because one has not the willingness to hear what is said, being overzealous to give the remedy before knowing what the illness is.

Neither does acceptance mean that the therapist makes himself merely a passive vessel ready to receive everything the sufferer may wish to pour in day after day. Much has been said about "the art of listening" and it has been needed; but there is the neurotic sufferer who wants nothing so much as a private audience with some person who will never tire of hearing the story of his sufferings retold, and who will listen to a mass of details which help the sufferer to shield himself from his own basic problem. The therapist is little interested in that endless circular retelling of the same story. He is concerned, certainly, with the sufferer's feelings, but he knows that these feelings already form a vicious circle and he desires to help him break out of that circle. He does not sit and merely listen as if hearing had virtue in itself. He responds, asks questions, comments; in a word, he participates emotionally with the sufferer as together they work deeper and deeper down into underlying strata of feelings and emotions.

Here we come upon a divergence of view among psychiatrists as to the questions concerning the sufferer which the therapist needs to have answered. Some believe that a thorough case history is necessary. Not only so, but in the analytical approach the attempt is made to aid in the bringing up of every particle of relevant experience out of the past, especially material which had been repressed into the unconscious.

In this conception of therapy, acceptance seems to imply that the therapist, in order to reach full effectiveness, must know as far as possible the entire personality. This method must be judged in the light of its achievements, and it may prove to be true that there are some forms of human suffering which can be got at in no other way.

Others, however, do not regard it as essential that the therapist should know the entire personality of the sufferer. Some would go so far as to say that it would not be essential that he should fully know even a small part of the personality. He accepts what is brought to him out of the depths of that personality, but many therapists who hold this conception do not regard it as their role to probe further into areas of experience which the individual does not of his own accord bring out. The questions then have to do with the meaning *to the sufferer* of the material which he has already brought forth. As that material itself is discussed with full acceptance, the sufferer will bring out still more if he feels it is needed and to the extent that he feels he is still being accepted.

Thus he, and not the therapist, remains in full control of the relationship and the depths and areas into which it will be carried. He is never pressed with searching questions about matters the discussion of which he himself has or has not initiated. He is not asked whether he has done this or that act in the past. Leading questions about his motives are not put to him. He is never urged to undress himself psychically in the presence of a greedy inquisitor who, as therapist, might take advantage of the situation to satisfy even scientific curiosity. Acceptance then in this conception has to do with as much of the self as the sufferer sees fit to bring into the relationship, but he and always he alone is left the judge of how much that will be.

TRANSFERENCE

As the re-living of the conflict goes forward, and as genuine acceptance is felt, another and new kind of emotion is commonly aroused in the sufferer himself. At last he has found one person who accepts him just as he is, guilt, anxiety, hostility, and all. To that person—that is, to the therapist—he begins to respond with a warm and strong feeling unlike any he has known before. It is trust, because he has brought out the dangerous thing that threatened him within, has put it in another's keeping, and has not been betrayed. It is confidence, because this therapist has been able to do what no other has ever yet done, and heaven knows enough others have tried it. It is love, yet not a love between equals, for this has in it something of the clinging to a stronger hand, at least until one is able to go alone. But it is a new kind of love, because it is born out of a new kind of self-respect; one cannot love in this manner when the self is held contemptible in its own eyes or in the eyes of others. It is a new kind of love, too, because the sufferer has found the therapist capable of accepting even hostility which burst out at him as the new self of the sufferer was emerging.

The Freudians have called this new feeling which develops within the sufferer toward the therapist as therapy proceeds, "transference." It was discovered that during the long process of psychoanalysis there was a "transference" to the physician. Transference is regarded as a displacement of infantile impulses onto the analyst, and the latter is made the object of both hostility and affection. This transference involves both positive and negative elements; in the former case the patient conceives a deep emotional attachment to the analyst, and in the latter, an equally deep antagonism toward him. In simpler words, the patient in successful analysis falls in love with the analyst, and yet may experience hate toward him. It would appear that in unsuccessful analysis the hate and resistance are triumphant.

During the progress of therapy the transference may pass through stages marked by great intensity of feeling. The patient may send his physician missives which could only be called love letters. A child or even a maturer person may display much anxiety over the possibility that any other person may hold a place in relation to the therapist like his own. He may say that he wishes to keep on coming to the therapist indefinitely. The dependence and jealousy thus shown are to be regarded as evidence of the intensity of the new feeling aroused. They are stages in growth only as they are left behind.

Re-birth

As the conflict is lived through in a relationship where the sufferer is accepted, and as an affection new in his own experience is aroused, the sufferer himself commences to feel that he is no longer the same person he was. A different self is coming into being. One psychiatrist when asked, "What is therapy?" replied, "The best way I know to describe it is in religious terms. It is being born again." Perhaps this is not common language among psychiatrists, and it is easy to understand that many of them would prefer other terms for the sake of avoiding confusion between religious and psychological thought.

The fact that the term "re-birth" itself is not commonly met in psychiatry need not concern us as long as a more important fact is seen: as therapy succeeds, the therapist is often told in symbolical acts or language that a previous self is passing away—death—and that a new one is being brought into life—re-birth, or resurrection.

This is expressed, naturally, in the greatest variety of ways. In the case of Mike Osborne, for example, it will be remembered that the killer doll became a sprightly dancer in expressing the fact that an inward change was taking place, and Mike said, "My snowball is getting bigger; it's nearly big enough now." Mrs. Osborne in describing Mike at a later time said, "He's ninety per cent different now."

Some will make it evident by a symbolical remark that they are aware of the new self emerging. Thus one woman coming to the end of therapy said, "Winter dies hard when Spring is coming, doesn't it?" Others may suggest that they now have a different view of the self, or of the world, or of both. At times it is said directly and rather prosaically: "The whole world looks different now; I feel like an explorer entering a new world."—"I feel so differently about everything now, that I don't even mind being as tall as I am." At other times the meaning may be left in symbols for those who can to understand; thus a girl who had been a prostitute was nearing the end of therapy and when the psychiatrist entered the room where she was waiting he found her drawing on the blackboard, making a rainbow with colored chalk, and singing a quiet little song. It was after the storm for her, and a new day had dawned.

Responsibility

The less one shows himself capable of managing his own life adequately, the more advice he is likely to receive. Both the neurotic and the delinquent have been flooded with advice. In each such case it is probable that they began to receive it much faster than they could assimilate it in early life, and that as the years went on the dosage increased heavily. It must seem to them as if every individual they encounter has a recipe for success and is trying with vigorous determination to enforce it upon them.

By the time he comes to any therapist, if he should seek such aid, it is rather probable that he has gone toward one or the other of two extremes. On the one hand he may have learned to lean on the advice of respected persons. In that event he always has someone else to blame if things go wrong again. On the other hand he may preserve a fragile sort of independence even in his neuroticism or his delinquency, by asking advice in order not to follow it. Such a person may come truculently, perhaps saying, "I want to get *your* view of my case. What do you think I ought to do?" What he really means is, "I just hope you, too, will put out some advice so I can refuse to keep it." This person is willing even to pay a fee for the privilege of defying advice.

Remember that in either case, whether as neurotic or as delinquent, in high probability he is a person with unmanageable hostility which is being directed toward himself or toward others. In the one case responsibility is being evaded. In the other it is being asserted, and asserted defiantly and for the sake of preserving the vicious circle of aggression in which he is already entrapped. This being so the therapeutic relationship takes on a large part of its distinctive character from the fact that the therapist will not assume responsibility which belongs to the sufferer, not even a minute part of it.

This is so different from all that the sufferer has heretofore encountered as to startle and often confuse him. The relationship is put on a distinctive footing the moment the therapist says, "I do not have any advice to give you." Many persons, either misunderstanding the nature of this relationship or afraid of it, will leave in order to seek plain and definite advice elsewhere, which can always be plentifully secured.

If the relationship does not break down at this point, the therapist is likely to begin by utilizing some situation, however simple, in which a choice must be made then and there. In the clinic, for example, an individual is often confronted with the choice of an hour on the schedule for his next appointment, or with the decision whether he shall sign his name with pen or pencil, and so on. Often an individual who has gained a reputation for brazen aggression will seem completely bewildered before so simple a choice and may take an unbelievable length of time in coming to his decision.

In this and all other comparable passages between sufferer and therapist where the former confronts a decision which *he* must make and which no other will make for him, there may be the first birth pains of a self now beginning to act on its own responsibility. Such choices as these, of course, are but a beginning, and require to be followed by other choices having larger and still larger significance. But it is not too much to say in psychology that the first assumption of genuine responsibility coincides with the re-birth of a self; and in the case of a person who has already established an inadequate pattern of living it may mark the beginning of the death of an old self and the rising of a new one.

In regard to questions of responsibility the difference between the approach in psychiatry and that often found in religion are perhaps as great as in any other respect. There is one point especially in which the ordinary procedure of a minister raises a serious problem in therapy. It is not enough merely to say that in his pastoral relationships the minister finds it excessively difficult to refrain from giving advice, although this certainly is true. More important is the fact that with many ministers there is a deep conviction that it is their duty to give definite advice to parishioners in general, and in particular to those who come for pastoral counsel. Here it is not possible to speak in general terms which are equally applicable to all ministers and to all religious bodies.

It is well known that some ministers decline to become a conscience for other men, and by cultivating individual responsibility endeavor also to cultivate personal growth. With many others, however, it is not so, and it is not uncommon to hear of ministers to whom it is a matter of much satisfaction that so great a number of individuals seek them out for advice, hang upon their words of counsel, and depend upon them for continued guidance.

The experience of the clinic seems to imply that those ministers, whatever their creed or church, who assume the responsibility for moral decisions on the part of their people tend to keep those persons spiritually immature, to say the least, and at the worst to render them the more helpless in proportion as the dangers confronted are the more serious.

COMPREHENSION

When such profound changes as we have been discussing take place, persons who are old enough and intelligent enough to do so are likely to look back over the course of personal life history with a twofold purpose. They wish to understand what caused the vast difficulties under which they were laboring, and they wish to understand how they were healed. Psychiatrists differ greatly in the degree of importance they attach to the sufferer's comprehension of his own situation, as a factor in therapy.

In the earlier scientific work on nervous and mental diseases, delinquency, and criminology, attention was given very largely to causes. This was the more natural since all these phenomena, so senseless when viewed in a rational light, had always baffled the comprehension of the wisest. When it began to be believed that some of the causes which had hitherto eluded discovery were now coming to light, all the enthusiasm of the explorer was aroused.

Thus in the earlier published work on nervous and mental illnesses the thought as expressed is largely confined to diagnosis. As a background for the diagnosis it was the custom to gather exhaustive case histories intended to be so thorough that no important detail would escape. In psychiatry the emphasis upon inquiry into causes received added weight from the work of Freud. Believing as he did that neurotic illness developed out of repression, and that repression in its turn involved the unconscious, it was incumbent upon him to investigate the unconscious. That process as Freud developed it was exceedingly lengthy, a hundred to five hundred hours of interview, for example, not being unusual in this method of treatment of one patient.

To put it in the briefest compass, Freud held that the neurotic patient required an understanding of the causes of his own illness if he were to recover. In such a view a therapist would be essentially a person who is trained to help a sufferer understand the true nature of the causes underlying his condition. In that event it would be said that the patient heals himself, and the therapist's skill consists to no small degree in his ability to allow the patient to do so, that is, to find for himself a new and better way to surmount the barriers in himself and in his environment which until now have thwarted him and begun to destroy him.

A Therapeutic Relationship

The question is now being asked by persons outside the Freudian movement, whether therapy is due to the fact that the patient comprehended the nature of his suffering, or whether it is due primarily to his emotional relationship with the therapist.

One may now clearly discern the emergence of a view whose general tenor is that therapy takes place in a controlled relationship with a suitable person.[3] This is a profounder conception by far than the one which holds that the sufferer from guilt may be released from his guilt by a rational comprehension of the reasons why he feels guilty. For it does not recreate the old dichotomy between reason and emotion which we have seen running through so much human thought from Plato to Freud. Instead, it locates the feeling factors of therapy in the very area of experience where the deeper layers of guilt, anxiety, and hostility arise; that is, in the feelings and emotions themselves.

The therapist then, in this view, is a person with whom the sufferer from guilt, anxiety, and hostility can enter an emotional relationship. The nature of this relationship is new in the experience of the neurotic or the delinquent, supplying some emotional element in experience which hitherto he has lacked, enabling him to break the bonds which heretofore have held him.

Reduced to the simplest possible terms, then, it can be said that the sense of guilt arose out of dynamic but malignant human relationships, and may be relieved by entering another dynamic but controlled relationship with a suitable person who is the therapist.

THE THERAPIST

How can we account for what happens in a sufferer when therapy succeeds? We have just been saying that in his relationship with the therapist he re-lives his emotional conflict, is accepted for exactly what he is, displaces both his hostility and his love onto the therapist, experiences what is for him a new kind of love toward another person, finds a new self coming into being within himself, and begins to accept responsibility for himself. But why do these revolutionary changes take place within him?

In order to get at the root of the matter it is necessary now to go back and pick up again an earlier consideration which was left incomplete. We pointed out that the first love an individual experiences toward another person in his most dynamic relationships is of an Eros character. We were at pains to point out that Eros love is love which has the motive of protecting and enhancing the standing of the self. Eros love cannot grow into something yet richer unless it is thwarted, but when it is thwarted hostility is aroused. The hostility thus aroused can be managed within the early dynamic relationships if it is met within those relationships by Agape love. But in proportion as the hostility is not thus met it tends to produce anxiety and guilt feelings which may become destructive. This much we have already developed at some length.

The person whom we have been calling the sufferer is one who has been going through just such an emotional experience, for a few months or for many years as his case may be; and there he is, dead-locked, caught in a blind alley from which he cannot extricate himself. He cannot get beyond Eros love in his human relationships. It is not that he does not love, for he loves intensely, but with a kind of love which can only imprison him the more relentlessly. If his character tends generally toward that of the neurotic, he loves his suffering, devotes himself to it with a strange passion, and is de-stroying himself by it. If his character tends generally toward the antisocial, such as in delinquent and criminal persons, he exists by the use of his hostility, perhaps even loves that hostility. He devotes himself to his aggression, and perhaps destroys both himself and others by it.

And here we come to the crucial point. In truly effective therapy the sufferer has encountered Agape love toward himself from another person. Agape love, as was earlier said, is love which has the motive of enhancing the standing of another person and liberating him into true personality and individuality. The form of Agape love whch he encounters now, coming to him from the therapist, enables him to satiate his own Eros love, dispose of his own hostility, anxiety, and guilt, and respond with Agape love. The guilt, anxiety, and hostility which arose in a malignant human relationship characterized by Eros love, have been disposed of in another dynamic but therapeutic relationship characterized by Agape love.

But there is still more. Consider the case of two persons who are bound together by hostility in a dynamic relationship such as that between mother and child. If both of them can experience effective therapy, the malignant nature of the relationship between them may be transformed, so that it will begin to take on the character of Agape love, and both these individuals who have been linked together in mutual destruction begin now to help liberate each other into free personality. This was exemplified in the case of the Osbornes, as will be recalled.

For clarity's sake we again summarize the things we have said at length in attempting to describe a journey tortuous to those whose lot it is to go that way. Guilt, anxiety, and hostility, that trio of destroyers, arise in the most dynamic relationships when those relationships are suffused with Eros love. They may be disposed of in a dynamic relationship when Eros love, empty-handed love, is transcended by Agape love, the love which sets one free. The therapist, not merely because of his technical training, but more important, because of his own character, is a person who is capable of bringing that Agape factor into a relationship. The result of effective therapy is that the vicious circle of destructive Eros love is broken by introducing Agape love into human relationships.

◄ VI ►

THE CROSS OF CHRIST

WE HAVE BEEN looking intently into a microcosm, the tiny but turbulent world of one individual with his hostility, his anxiety, and his guilt. But that one individual is a world figure. His plight was as familiar in ancient Nineveh and Athens as it is in modern New York or Berlin, and doubtless it will be so in those unknown cities of the long future. We turn now directly to the question, "What has Christianity for him?"

Christianity is a breath-taking religion when one senses the enormous sweep of its conceptions, the depth of its insight, and the daring of its proposals. The moment one touches Christianity with any seriousness he must be prepared to find that on the one hand it subjects the human individual to a scrutiny as minute as that of any psychologist, and that on the other hand it is satisfied with nothing less than a complete philosophy of the entire universe not only for all time but for eternity as well.

As for the things that chiefly concern us in these lectures, these general statements may be made at once by way of orienting ourselves as to the thought which is to follow. Christianity interprets God, the universe, and man in such a way as to transcend the dilemma which has haunted man from the beginning of recorded history as to the responsibility for his plight. The proposal which it makes as a way of transcending the dilemma is meant to be realizable in human experience, and is meant to result in complete freedom from guilt, anxiety, and hostility. And it has established a form of society meant to produce and nurture persons all of whose guilt, anxiety, and hostility can be absorbed as rapidly as they arise;

with the frankest recognition that this end so greatly to be desired will never be fully achieved in time; and yet it is capable of dealing with that hard fact of human experience in such a way as to triumph over it. These statements are not intended as so many points to be treated one by one. They are more in the nature of four threads—God, Jesus Christ, Spirit, and human relationships— no one of which will long be absent from view in the following material.

Are we now leaving the clinic? Not in the least, except as it may seem so to any whose passion is more for the phrases that describe reality than it is for reality itself. The vocabulary, indeed, changes in part as we go from psychology to theology. Many of the events to be considered move out far beyond the walls of any interviewing room. The Deity, not the therapist, now confronts us. But the human creature with his hostility, anxiety, and guilt remains. And as concerns this human sufferer it will be our thesis that three propositions are true. The therapy which the psychiatrist effects with a necessarily limited few is offered to all men everywhere upon the observance of certain conditions. The meaning which those conditions have for human experience is illuminated by therapy. And Christianity puts its offer to heal the guilt of man in a cosmic and eternal framework, as psychiatry by its own nature cannot do.

The Human Dilemma Transcended

Man is a creature of conflict, we have been saying throughout these lectures; such he is now, and such he has been. And as has already been said, the human dilemma concerning responsibility for the outcome of his conflict is this. If the final responsibility is within man himself, the result is pessimism of a dye so deep that the best escape from the plight is flight from the body or flight into destruction. But if the responsibility is outside of man, whether in God or in environment, the result is a universe of Nonsense which one endures as best he can, depending upon his mood, until his little day is ended. In neither case does the indefinite prolonging of life —immortality—present an alluring prospect. One span of life, on earth, is enough.

In Christianity it is commonly held that the responsibility is within man himself. Every possible escape from this hard conclusion seems hedged about in Christian teaching. It is hardly necessary even to recall the characteristic emphases of Christian doctrine regarding man's responsibility, so familiar are they. What of man?

He is responsible for the outcome of his conflict; from him is taken the satisfaction of sitting in judgment on any other man, for it is his own condition which requires judging. *He* is the sinner, and the wages of sin is death. *He* is responsible for the plight into which his own sins have brought him. *He* is even accounted responsible with a kind of cumulative responsibility which reaches into the past and takes in his heredity. *He* is blocked off from attributing the blame for his own situation to his fathers or to their fathers before them. More yet, *he* is even held accountable, in many lines of Christian thought, for the sins of the fathers themselves, as when it was said by Jesus that the blood of all the prophets slain from the foundation of the world shall be required of *this* generation.[1] Thus when to the teaching that every man is a sinner are added the yet more difficult doctrines of original sin, little more remains to be said by way of a reminder here that in Christianity the responsibility is held to be within man himself. And yet it means but little in Christianity to say that man is responsible, for man is responsible *to God*. In Christianity, as indeed in Judaism and Islam as well, man is under the judgment of God. He is a sufferer, but he is more than that, he is an offender. It is the will or the law *of God* which he has not kept.

Beneath a difference in terminology this view is present in the teaching both of Jesus and of Paul, to speak now of no others. In the former it appears in the doctrine of the Kingdom; that is, the Kingship or Lordship of God. Here every soul is confronted with the standing claim of God upon a man's supreme loyalty, devotion, and obedience. Until that claim of God upon him is acknowledged, a man is "lost" to God. In Paul it appears, for example, in his doctrine of universal guilt, as when he says, "Now we know that what things soever the law saith, it saith to them who are under the law: that every mouth may be stopped, and all the world [*cosmos*] may become guilty [under judgment] before God."[2]

By all such teaching Christianity signifies that the decisions a man reaches in his conflict are not only a concern of that man himself in his own privacy; they are of concern in the entire universe. Whatever else a man's sin may be in addition, it begins and ends by being sin against God. "Law" in Christianity means something so profound that the breaking of it not only brings injury and destruction to the guilty person himself; but more than that, it thrusts out a disturbing factor whose ever-widening circles eventually reach to the limits of the universe itself. Christianity, by its doctrine of man under the judgment of God, is saying that the outcome of one's individual life is not a matter of indifference in a morally neutral universe. Rather, the hurt of a man in his prison is also the hurt of God in His heaven.

The Christian doctrine of divine judgment as expressed in the New Testament has two aspects, not always easy to distinguish in the literature, but both essential to an understanding of the New Testament view of God's nature, man's guilt, and divine redemption. In the first of these aspects the judgment of God is here and now, at any moment which one can call "the present." In the other it is yet to come, always impending but always still in the

future. That is to say, the human conflict whose outcome leads to
the necessity of judgment is not suddenly ended once for all, either
in an individual or in society. No Utopia is promised; on the contrary, conflict is seen as pervading all human life as long as that life
endures, until that vague but cataclysmic day when the Kingdom
of God is made complete.

Here is religious realism of the first rank, concerning both human
nature and human society. The human scene will not suddenly be
transformed into a paradise. It is constantly under divine judgment
as imperfect, so that all evasions may be swept away, and all
subterfuges invaded, to the end that black may stand out as black
and nothing else against the white of perfect righteousness and
moral holiness.

Yet the human scene is always under the divine yearning as well
as under the divine judgment. That momentous insight, so variously
and so richly expressed in Christian thought, provides precisely the
basis from which Christianity transcends the human dilemma
already so often mentioned. The basis of redemption, the ground
of hope as against a flight into Nonsense or self-destruction, lies in
the paradoxical nature of God Himself. The incredible gospel of
Christianity, its tremendous Good News, is that God Himself in
human form has come into the human scene, has stood and still
stands not against but beside man in his human plight, has suffered
and died not only for man but with man, to the end that any who
will may be liberated into a new life which is nothing less than a
rising from the dead. This Good News is summed up in the death
and resurrection of Jesus Christ, a scandal to reason, but the power
of God to them that believe *in Him*.

We have now to inquire how the gospel of the coming, the life,
the suffering, the death, and the resurrection of the Christ becomes
or may become "the power of God" for the liberation of man from

his guilt, his anxiety, and his hostility. The field of material relevant to this inquiry is enormous, including no less than the entire range of Christian theology from the earliest New Testament writings to the latest book on the subject today. But within this vast area certain trunk lines of Christian experience and thought may be discerned. It will be our purpose to seek them. This may be done by first considering how Jesus dealt with guilt and related questions during His own ministry, and then asking how Christians approached these same questions afterward, when there had been time enough to reflect upon the cosmic import of the mission and message of Jesus Christ.

THE EARTHLY JESUS

The Incarnation. From the earliest records of Christianity which we possess it is possible to get factual data concerning the life and ministry of Jesus, but something else also lies there which is equally, if not even more, important. For those same records tell us something of what He meant to His earliest followers. And from the outset it is apparent in these records that the first Christians of whom we have any knowledge saw in Jesus one who was truly a man, but not merely a man. They received Him as a personality absolutely unique in all history.

The problem of defining this personality and of explaining its relationship with God evidently became acute as soon as His impact upon men began to be felt, and afterward was unremittingly toiled upon for centuries; indeed, in one form or another it is never long absent from Christian history. The doctrine that developed is in itself a subject of specialized study in theology. We must be content here with the modest aim of pointing out two great convictions among early Christians. Then we may attempt to show something of the meaning which these convictions had as far as redemption from guilt is concerned.

The Jewish people, who had known so many frustrations of personal and national life, were in expectation of a Deliverer. In their own tongue they spoke of this Deliverer as the "Messiah," and in using the Greek language they referred to Him as the "Christ." Both terms, Messiah and Christ, meant the "Anointed," that is, one who stood in a peculiar relationship to God, was set aside for His particular task as deliverer of His people, and was empowered with all that was necessary for the performance of His task. The first great conviction of early Christians concerning Jesus was that He is the Messiah, the Christ, the Anointed, the Deliverer of the people of God. This conviction shows with especial clarity in the first three Gospels, in the Acts, and wherever the Christian message is directed primarily to the Jewish mind. As long as the Christian message was being proclaimed chiefly to the people of Jewish background, the conception of Jesus as Messiah served the Christian purpose admirably.

But the Christian church quickly broke out of the confines of Judaism, and heralded its message of redemption to Gentile as well as to Jew. The Gentile, too, often enough was looking for deliverance, but not against the same mental background as that of the Jew. The intellectual life of New Testament times, outside of Judaism, and even within it, was greatly influenced by Hellenic thought. Greek minds and all others saturated with Hellenic thought found the Jewish conception of Jesus as the Messiah difficult, not to say unintelligible. Thus as Christianity faced the first great test of its ability to cross racial barriers, the question was not only whether the social and emotional gulf between them could be bridged, but whether the great void between minds that thought differently could be bridged also.

This feat Christianity achieved by seizing upon the conception of Logos, a conception apparently as familiar to Hellenic minds as Messiah was to Jewish ones. Logos meant a principle inherent in the universe throughout all time and perpetually operative. It embodied such ideas as reason, order, divine will, wisdom, power, and creativeness. The second great conviction among early Christians concerning Jesus was that He is the Logos of God. This appears most plainly, of course, in the Gospel of John where the term Logos itself is used and is translated "Word"—"In the beginning was the Word, and the Word was with God, and the Word was God,"[3] and so on. In other New Testament writings the two conceptions of Jesus as the Christ of God, and Jesus as the Logos of God, play upon and influence each other until one imagines he can almost hear the quick pantings of the strenuous intellectual effort to weld these two conceptions into one still greater over-arching idea of Jesus which will be sufficient to do justice to all that He means for thought and experience.[4]

These two convictions among early Christians stand as a perpetual reminder that Jesus of Nazareth confronts man both as a datable fact in history and as a timeless fact in metaphysics, that is, the mental and emotional realm where truth is independent of time and place and therefore, if truth at all, is eternally true, the same yesterday, today, and forever. This double aspect of Jesus as a person, so early recognized in Christianity, had numerous consequences of greatest importance, as far as questions of guilt and redemption are concerned. Only three of them can here be taken under view.

One was the unfailing insistence that Jesus came forth from God as no other person ever had come or ever would come; and therefore that He spoke for God, acted for God, and manifested God through what He Himself was, as no other person ever had done or ever could do. The attempt to define the uniqueness of His person with logical precision proved both rewarding and disappointing. It was rewarding because the church thus not only kept but developed a sense of its own uniqueness in history, and preserved its own integrity in the midst of influences which otherwise would have destroyed it. It was disappointing because the more precise the definitions became the more unintelligible they grew for common people. One of the classic examples is the so-called Athanasian Creed from which the following words will serve as an example of the language:

> For the right Faith is that we believe and confess: that our Lord Jesus Christ, the Son of God, is God and Man; God of the Substance of the Father, begotten before the worlds: and Man, of the Substance of his Mother, born in the world . . . One: not by conversion of the Godhead into flesh: but by assumption of the Manhood into God . . . So God and Man is one Christ.
>
> Athanasian Creed, 30-37

By contrast with the precise and elaborate definitions of formal theology there is an impressive array of what we may call "short theologies" of Jesus in the New Testament, as there always has been in later times as well. Consider, for example, how all of the meanings of the Athanasian Creed are expressed less exactly but far more powerfully in the Benedictus through these words: "The dayspring from on high hath visited us."[5] These short theologies are quick, highly suggestive terms which catch up in one phrase one aspect of the incarnation and put that aspect in an unforgettable symbol. For instance, Jesus is "The Son of God," "The Son of Man," "The Lord," "The King of the Jews," "The Son of David," "Thy Holy Child Jesus," "The Prophet of Nazareth," "The Holy One of God," "The Son of the Highest," "The Prince of Life," "A Prince and a Saviour," "The Just One," "The Lamb of God," "The Faithful and True," "The Lord of Glory," and "King of Kings, and Lord of Lords." Some of these terms are spread through much of the New Testament and are constantly being encountered. Others occur but rarely, indicating the possibility that individual Christians in many cases summed up for themselves what the incarnation meant for them in one crisp, unforgettable symbol. But the constant insistence that Jesus came forth from God is nowhere more strikingly expressed than in one of the names given Him, "Emmanuel," that is, "God with us."

Because Jesus was "God with us," the next consequence was the equally incredible assertion that in Jesus, God had gone down into the midst of man's plight and had shared it with him to the utmost. By being born of a woman and traversing the span of life from infancy to the death of a mature man, He had tasted alike the joy and the bitterness of living, with its love and with its hostility also. He had been tempted, they pointed out, at every place where He bore a likeness to us. But there was far more yet. He had not only shared the realm of life, but He had also shared the realm of death. Language groaned under the effort to explain what this might mean. Two great ideas stand out concerning it in the New Testament. He died *for* us, that is to say, with variant emphasis, He died on our behalf, in our stead, as our substitute, as the sacrificial victim offered in our place and for our sins. And He died *with* us, in such manner that He and we die jointly to an old life and jointly rise to a new one. All these meanings and others besides were gathered up in that later tremendous phrase of the Creed: "he descended into hell."

Because He came forth from God and because He went down into the hell of man's sin, yet another consequence was that He revealed through Himself, as never elsewhere in all history, what the *character* of God is. God is Agape—Love—and the cross not only demonstrates what that means, but also demonstrates that an inexhaustible supply of it is available in our universe. Here on a cosmic scale Agape love had broken through the vicious circle of man's self-destroying Eros love, and was forever available now to any man to liberate him from his own hostilities, to relieve his anxieties, and to carry away his guilt.

The records of Jesus' own ministry to men need to be read against a background of such ideas as we have just been discussing. For the four Gospels themselves were written, so to speak, in order to show that actual flesh and blood underlay a metaphysical conception of redemption which, without such detail, might quickly have evaporated into a cloud of glowing but nebulous formulas. Jesus came preaching, teaching, and healing. How did these bear upon guilt and upon its underlying causes?

Preaching. As I have shown elsewhere in some detail,[6] analysis of the first three Gospels makes it clear that the "preaching" of Jesus was not the rather omnibus activity which is now often designated by that term. It had a specific content, called the "Gospel." This "Gospel" was the Good News that the Kingdom of God is here, at hand. That was an indirect way of proclaiming that at long last the awaited Deliverer, the Christ, had come. News of that kind, announced at that time and to that people, would produce an electric effect which will be more readily understood by any who have awaited the announcement of some modern D-Day. The signal, simple in itself, stood for a momentous impending change in human affairs which had become intolerable.

Evidently Jesus made it clear at the beginning of His ministry, from what the Christ was able to deliver men. For example, Luke records that in Jesus' very early sermon at Nazareth He read from the prophet Isaiah these words: "The Spirit of the Lord is upon me, because he hath anointed me to preach the gospel to the poor; he hath sent me to heal the brokenhearted, to preach deliverance to the captives, and recovering of sight to the blind, to set at liberty them that are bruised, to preach the acceptable year of the Lord."[7] This language is still figurative in part, but when the full story of His mission has been told it is plain that He counted no human ill of any sort, whether physical, nervous, mental, social, economic, or political, as being beyond the range of the gospel's power to invade and conquer. *How* this might be so then became the subject of His teaching.

Teaching. If there is one theme that runs through all the recorded teaching of Jesus, that theme is the Kingdom of God. Of the meaning of that Kingdom we have already spoken in part, saying that it is the King*ship* of God over the individual—the estate or condition a man is in when God and God alone is his Sovereign, his Lord, his Ruler. But *then,* having once bowed his heart to acknowledge allegiance to One infinitely greater than himself, a man finds himself no mere subject of a monarch, but instead, he becomes a child of "our Father in heaven."

From this basis, by this pole star for all orienting, Jesus works out into the sea of human affairs. But there is to be no mistaking what the direction of this journey is: "Seek ye *first* the kingdom of God, and his righteousness." By this pole star, for example, one is oriented in relation to his fellows, his "brothers," the other sons of the Father. Perhaps the most searching parts of Jesus' ethic are His questions concerning what is constructive and what is damaging, as between men who are brothers.

Thus Jesus stripped away all that was non-essential in the busy traffic between men and God, showed where the trunk lines lay, and brought us to see what was essential: first and greatest of all, that a man should love God with every capacity he possesses; and second, that he should love his neighbor with a love as great as the self-love which each of us has. Upon these two supreme commandments hang all that was said in the Law or by the prophets.

What then is guilt in the eyes of God? God is not concerned, Jesus showed, over the kind of rubbish which a religion piles up as it ages, its fussy little laws and lawlets with their subdivisions and exceptions, so seriously promulgated and so seriously observed, its hair-splitting distinctions between the right and the wrong way of performing a ceremony, or hallowing the Sabbath, or fulfilling an obligation. These are not what "sin" means to Jesus, and the guilt which puts millstones around a man's neck arises from no such trifles in the cosmos as these. Sin, to Jesus, was whatever kept a man out of love with God and one's fellows. As long as a man carried hostility, his hostility was the seed-bed of his sin, as the teaching concerning forgiveness of our fellows shows. It would accomplish nothing under heaven except a lie, to declare a man guiltless and sign him with holy gestures in token of his absolution, as long as his hatred of his brother still rotted him inwardly.

Or as long as a man was anxious, his anxiety was a signal saying he could not yet trust God fully. For Jesus knew, as well as any modern does, what it feels like to be very small in a terrifying world. The *objects* of anxiety, Jesus frankly said, were needed things, but the "basic anxiety" could not be healed except by "basic trust" in a God whom one knows as truly a Father.

But what, when a man had at last found the way by trusting this Teacher and this teaching, and had begun to be truly a child of God, hostility emptied out, anxiety healed, and guilt carried away? Would he find in Jesus a new drillmaster to replace the ones he had left? Never. "What do *you* want?" He would begin to ask a fledgling disciple. He drove men to that hardest task, the making up of their own minds concerning the right and wrong of their own conduct, declining to be a divider of their disputed property, an arbiter of their tax problems, or even a prop to His mother when she was hungry for affection. By Him they would be judged at the end, whether or not they had learned to see the sick, the hungry, and the prisoner as with His eyes. But He would be no taskmaster standing by to whip them on in the performing of love's dear offices.

What have we in sum, but this: if a man's first and greatest privilege is sonship to the Father in the Kingdom of God, the absence of the love to God which is his highest right in the universe is the final root of all his other hostility, anxiety, and guilt. The bottom of a man's hell is a malignant relationship with God. In that breeding ground his other poisons spawn, and from it they spread.

Since a man's most fundamental discord is in his relationship with God, and since his malignant relationships with his fellows both flow from and further aggravate his already diseased relationship with God, two tempting remedies for the ills that beset him are ruled out. He will not be cured by tinkering with the environment, setting up a "new social order" as we call it now. Surely this must be the meaning when Jesus steadily refuses to deliver His people by establishing a political "new deal" in Judea. Neither could a man be healed of his basic disharmony by becoming a more ardent religionist. Jesus knew, as any psychiatrist today knows, that frightened people were wearing themselves out in religious busyness because they could not endure to meet God and be inwardly transformed. These were the "Pharisees" of that or any other day, who by means of religion had barricaded themselves against God.

The radical cure that was possible could take place only if the root of the trouble could be reached. What this involves is variously expressed. A man devoting his best energies to his own welfare, seeking in Eros love to "save his own life," would have to break his own self-protecting shell; perhaps by giving away his wealth, as with the rich young man; or abandoning his present calling, as with Matthew; or forgetting his own devices for gaining prestige and saving his own skin, as with Peter. Again, it would be said that he required a different "heart," for a man was defiled only by what came out of his own heart, and what issued from the heart could not be different until the heart itself was different. Or yet again, a man could not enter the Kingdom until he put an end to the process of growing old in the wrong direction, reversed the "normal" course of his "growth" and turned back the clock to start anew, becoming as a little child, or even being born again.

Here then, with such rich imagery, is the same vicious circle of Eros love which, Jesus proposes, can be broken; and through that rift in self-love God can get to a man. But how can it be broken? That is most sharply seen in the healing ministry of Jesus.

Healing. Deliverance, in Jesus' ministry, meant healing the bodies as well as the souls of men. Hardly a page of the Gospels can be turned without coming upon the subject of healing: "And they brought unto him all sick people that were taken with divers diseases and torments";[8] or, "And when he saw him, he fell at his feet, and besought him greatly, saying, My little daughter lieth at the point of death: I pray thee, come and lay thy hands on her, that she may be healed; and she shall live. And Jesus went with him."[9]

The accounts of healing present many difficulties. Usually we know the condition only by the popular name given it some two thousand years ago, and therefore we have an unsatisfactory basis for comparison with diseases as described in modern medicine. And since we seldom can know exactly what the condition was, it is difficult to make satisfactory comparison with modern means of healing. For example, we do not know precisely what is meant by "leprosy"; we naturally assume it to be the same as we know now by that name, but this is not necessarily true, for in Jewish thought the walls of a house could show the symptoms of leprosy, when possibly something like mildew is meant.[10]

The difficulties are especially great in connection with any accounts of healing where the condition appears to have had an infectious origin or an organic basis. It is rather common knowledge now, of course, that persons may suffer hysterical conditions such as lameness, paralysis, blindness, speechlessness, and so on, without any known physical impairment of body or organs. Relief is possible by therapy without medicine and operations. But the distinctions between "functional" and "organic" conditions seem less important as psychosomatic medicine advances.

Again, there is the very frequent mention of persons possessed with demons, unclean spirits, and so on. In many instances it is entirely reasonable to regard these as being descriptive of persons such as we now call neurotic or psychotic. This is not altogether satisfactory since Matthew appears to separate the "lunatick" from those possessed with devils,[11] but the description of a "lunatick" which he gives elsewhere suggests epilepsy.[12] But when allowance is made for the fact of popular speech and unscientific conceptions, there is to say the least a good probability that "demon possession" is the general equivalent of "nervous and mental diseases."

We have, then, the picture of a mass of suffering persons seeking Jesus in order to be healed. The nature of their troubles is none too clear. The thing that stood out to all the writers of the Gospels was that *Jesus healed.* And Jesus Himself regarded His healing from two points of view that are most significant. One of these He put forward in argument. When people asked Him by what authority He cast out devils, His reply indicated that it was "with the finger of God";[13] that is to say, He could do this work because He had power *from God* for it. That was His theology of the matter, pointing to the ultimate source of healing, as of life itself.

But when He talked with one who sought to be healed, the emphasis sounds different. He may suggest one simple act as the beginning of a cure; at least twice He is recorded as telling a man, "Take up thy bed, and walk,"[14] or again He will say, "Stretch forth thy hand."[15] Was this, perhaps, inducing a man to do some least thing for himself in the area where he had lost all confidence in himself? However that may be, it is more significant yet that repeatedly He makes such statements as these to a person who is being restored: *"Thy faith* hath saved thee,"[16] or *"Thy faith* hath made thee whole,"[17] or "According to *your faith* be it unto you,"[18] or "Great is *thy faith*: be it unto thee even as thou wilt."[19] If we skirt around this emphasis upon what the *person himself feels and does* as an imperative step in recovery of body or soul, thereafter we shall be studying the play *Hamlet* with Hamlet himself left out. But what is this self-activity of the sufferer himself as he begins to be healed?

Repentance and Faith. A revolution in human affairs is highly complicated. A Victor Hugo, sensing the interplay of persons and forces, can write reams in describing a day or an hour during which the structure of society was taking a new form. When a political revolution is under view, we can often hit upon two events which seem to symbolize, respectively, the hauling down of an old flag and the running up of a new one. Thus in America there was the Declaration of Independence and the adoption of a new constitution. In France there was the fall of the Bastille and, similarly, the creation of a new constitution by the National Assembly. Picking out such turning points is a help to thought in that it provides simple points of reference; but that simplicity itself is deceptive if we suppose we have captured historical truth fully by means of a pair of convenient symbols.

The situation is comparable when a revolution takes place in the life of one person. Augustine, a master psychologist of the Christian soul, occupies the greater part of his long *Confessions* with a description of his own migration of spirit. But for the sake of clarity and simplicity we need terms, again, by which we may refer to the taking down of one flag and the putting up of another; the abandoning of an old way and the embracing of a new one. But when we have found the terms it is not to be supposed that they are more than convenient verbal counters to be used in referring to something which, in reality, may be highly complicated and saturated with feeling. Two words of exactly this character in the Christian speech are repentance and faith.

The point at which the shell of an individual's defenses begins to break is a time when that person is starting to "change his mind"; and repentance means just that: a change of mind, particularly about oneself. By the accidents of speech we never think of calling it "repentance" when a sufferer is re-evaluating his own self in his relationship with a therapist. We have reserved the word for religious speech, and there we commonly use it to mean "being sorry for sin." But in the New Testament it means vastly more than that. As Chamberlain expresses it, "When the New Testament calls for repentance it is demanding that we correct all our false notions of prayer, of righteousness, of life's objectives, of God and His Kingdom, of all ambitions and aspirations that are not in harmony with God's will. In other words, repentance is a revamping of the outlook and outreach of all life."[20]

Faith is the name given to the second aspect of the revolution in a self. When the shell of self-defenses has been shattered, one is becoming capable of both giving and receiving a new kind of love.

Christian faith commences at the moment when that affectionate trust begins to be given to Christ. But faith is more than the warm glow of a new kind of affection. It is confidence, at least strong enough to cause one to begin acting, even if that first act under the new Sovereign seems no more important than to "stretch forth thy hand." That, too, is "faith."

In the case of the ill, this "faith" was roughly comparable with what is now known as "transference" to the therapist. We can now say simply and without cant that during the healing ministry of Jesus the sick person fell in love with Jesus, and his "faith" healed him. And in principle it was exactly the same in the case of that yet greater number who sought deliverance from anxiety and guilt which did not put them in bed but which held them back from the good joys of living none the less surely. The "break-through" for these, just as for the ill abed, was the same at bottom: to burst the bonds of Eros love by repenting and responding to the Agape love in Christ. This is most forcefully brought out in the Gospel of John, where everything in a man's destiny turns on "believing in," or as it literally is, "believing into," Christ.[21]

THE COSMIC CHRIST

The magnitude of the love that was in Christ, its "breadth, and length, and depth, and height," could not be apprehended until His death had showed it forth more fully than His life could do. But the death of Christ was a stumbling block both for feeling and for reason. His own disciples at first could not accept it emotionally. The Jews could not square it with their conception of the Messiah. To the Greeks it was an intellectual scandal that the Son of God should die; and when to this was added the proclamation that the Son of God had not only died but then had risen from the dead, a Greek hearer knew nothing to do but to laugh and leave.

We have already said that the gospel as Jesus preached it meant that the Messiah, the Christ, had come. After Calvary and the empty tomb, the gospel became what it could not have been in that first preaching. Preaching the gospel in the early church meant the authoritative proclamation of a short body of momentous facts; Jesus Christ had come, had suffered, had died, and had risen from the dead.[22] Two things began to happen at the same time. One was a tremendous inrush of revolutionizing power in human lives as converts to the new gospel multiplied and as the young church grew. The other was the formulating of a rational explanation for this movement which was turning things upside down in religion, society, and politics. As far as intellectual issues are concerned, the crux of the matter lay in the death and resurrection. The world was familiar enough already with the idea that God could come into the human scene, and that part of the gospel presented men with no insurmountable difficulties. But the claim that He had died and risen again staggered the mind. Accordingly, the core of the earliest Christian theology inevitably had to do with the Cross.

That earliest theology, of course, is found as far as we know it in the New Testament; and there it is especially clear in the writings of Paul, the first three Gospels, the book of Acts, and the Johannine writings consisting of the Gospel and Epistles of John. All these are directed in one manner or another to giving a theology of the death and resurrection of Jesus. And we miss almost the entire force of what is said in these writings if we begin *first,* in examining them, to search for their theology of the atonement. They have that theology of the atonement, of course. But first and foremost they are a theology of faith; or, if one prefers not to obscure the differing emphases, they are theologies of faith. They give the meaning of the death and resurrection of Christ in order that *faith in Christ* may be kindled, to the end that a man may be saved by *believing in Christ* who died and rose again. They saw Him now, not merely as an earthly figure, but as a cosmic one. The redemption which He brought was available to man not only in Palestine during the days of His flesh; it was an eternal redemption, and it was available to any man in any age in any place.

Of the writings which we mentioned, the earliest Epistles of Paul appear to be the nearest in time to the days when Jesus lived in Galilee. Paul, having been trained as a Jewish rabbi, approaches the cross from the background of a Jew. He must know its relation to the great body of Jewish Law, which he had spent so large a part of his life studying and trying faithfully to observe. But the cross had revolutionized all his thinking about that Torah. Swept away now is his previous idea that a man would be saved by keeping the Law.

In consequence, his conception of guilt changes too. He can distinguish differing kinds of guilt. There are, for example, the Gentiles who know not the Law, even though they keep some of its precepts because "by nature" these are "written in their hearts."[23] There are the Jews who do have the Law and observe it more or less faithfully. But both Gentile and Jew are guilty. The crux of their guilt, in Paul's thought, has to do with a relationship with God, and not primarily a relationship to Law. With Paul guilt as fact and guilt as responsibility arise out of a malignant relationship with God, and the roots of guilt cannot be reached by being a good man, or by being faithful to any code of law—that is, by the "works of the law"; they can only be reached by a change in the emotional relationship with God.

For Paul faith in Christ marks the beginning of that change which, if the faith be "from the heart," will bring a man into a wholly new relationship with God. This new relationship in one of its aspects is called "justification" by Paul. Under another of its aspects a man's status in the new relationship with God is referred to as "adoption" into the family of God as a son, but Paul does not make much use of this term. He attaches the greatest importance to justification.

A man is not justified by works, he is justified by faith. Faith toward Christ or faith in Christ arises from man. "Justification" meets such a man from God. The verb "to justify" belongs in a class which grammarians call verbs of mental action. This particular mental action on the part of God signifies that God is receiving into the estate of sonship that man who believes in Christ. To say that God justifies a man is to say that God accepts that man as guiltless. God is receiving him, Paul never tires of urging, not because he has been so good a man and has kept the code of Jewish Law so faithfully; He is receiving him into sonship even though he be an evil man who has broken every law of God and of humanity; He is receiving him not because he has been a good man or an evil man, but only because he has *faith in Christ*. Given that starting point the man will become a new man whatever he may have been before.

As to the Gospels, we have already spoken at some length concerning their emphasis on faith. This emphasis becomes the more striking when we recall the well-known fact that the first three Gospels were written after the church was already in existence, and during a period when the meaning of faith in Christ greatly needed clarifying for those who were called upon to exercise it but had never known Jesus in human form. In the Acts, describing the earliest phase of the church, the same theme meets us as the story of Christian missionary activity unfolds: "Believe on the Lord Jesus Christ, and thou shalt be saved."[24] In the Johannine writings the theme of love is developed in a different and more explicit manner. A man believes into Christ and thus finds eternal life.

The one law within eternal life is love, and the theme is traced in every possible direction—love from God to man, love from man to God, love from Christ to man, love from the believer to Christ, and love between brethren.

Faith *in Christ,* then, is in all these writings the turning point in personal destiny. Even the shades of feeling arising as the new relationship is consummated are significant. Sometimes it is the "faith of Christ"; that is, the faith of which Christ is the object.[25] Again it will be "faith in Christ," as if to say that a man's faith arises because he is now within or a part of Christ.[26] Still again it may denote movement and action on the part of the believer who has faith *into* or believes *into* Christ,[27] or *upon* Christ.[28] Faith marks the break out of eternal death and the entrance then and there into eternal life.

If we pause now to see the place to which the thought has brought us it is this. In the earliest Christian theology the primal source of a man's hostility, his anxiety, and his guilt lies in a malignant relationship with God. He may be redeemed from that condition by entering into a new and different relationship with God, that of son to Father. This he can do by faith in Christ. Faith is the specific name given to a particular kind of relationship which a man may have with Jesus Christ. It is faith in *Him* as a *Person,* and is deeply colored by feeling, especially by confidence and love. Such faith when genuine begins to revolutionize character and produce a "new man."

THE DISPLACEMENT OF FAITH

The necessities of the early church led to the production of a theology of the cross in order to stir men to have faith in Christ who had died and risen again. The same necessities exist in principle now. And yet always, now as then, redeeming faith in Christ is constantly in danger of being rendered impotent or even of being destroyed by the two culturing mediums which are needed to keep it alive. One of these is theology, and the other is the church.

The displacement of faith from Christ as its object to theology as its object takes place so easily, so naturally, that one is scarcely able to put a finger upon the point at which the process begins. It seems ordinarily to start at some time when the integrity of the Christian message or of the church is threatened. At such a time many theologies of the cross may be competing for the attention of men. Each may claim to be inspired. The immature person is confused, not knowing which is a more dependable account of the cross. He does not know "what to believe." A revered man or council may speak to him, saying in effect, "This is the truth, believe this and be saved. Disbelieve this at the peril of your soul."

In principle this is just what happened early in the history of Christianity. Credal formulations begin to appear which express faith in Christ, and do it in terms which are acceptable to the authorities of the church as the right way of confessing faith in Christ. Then the credal statement itself becomes the test of a man's faith; "This is the right way—do you believe this?" This stage in the displacement of faith had been reached long before the time of the so-called Athanasian Creed, but that document is one of many which will illustrate the meaning of the faith which is demanded. "For the right faith is that we believe and confess that . . . this is the Catholic faith which, except a man believe truly and firmly, he cannot be saved." Centuries afterward a yet more peculiar stage has been reached. Doctrine is now stated in a negative form; an article of belief may be introduced by the phrase, "If anyone saith that . . ." such and such things are not true, and may end with the phrase, "let him be anathema."

This displacement of faith from Christ to theology concerning Christ may well be considered the most serious heresy in Christianity, for it strikes at the root of the very thing it seeks to protect, and does it under the banner of love and devotion. It has the sound of deep piety, for it states its case under the name of orthodoxy—for the defense of "the faith" and other such high phrases. It first came forth in the Catholic Church, but it constantly makes its appearance in Protestantism also. Wherever a theory of the Person of Christ, or of the atonement, or any other doctrine concerning Him is made the test of a man's fitness to be in the Kingdom of God, there the kiss of betrayal has been openly given. It was their doctrine concerning the Christ which led Jesus Himself to say to the Pharisees of His own day, "For ye shut up the kingdom of heaven against men: for ye neither go in yourselves, neither suffer ye them that are entering to go in."[29]

And lest this all be taken as referring only to "other men" it should be said that this lecture itself will still further illustrate the easy possibility of an unintended displacement of faith. If it has value at all, that value will lie in the stimulating of faith *in Christ,* and not in a theory about faith or about Christ. The theory itself— that is, the doctrine here being expressed—is fallible, open to correction, and easily abandoned if untrue. If true faith in Christ is stimulated, that faith will be saving faith. This last statement itself is again a doctrine, stated in the earnest conviction that it is true; but its truth does not depend upon the one stating it, for one who wishes to do so can try it and determine for himself whether it is true. If he should find that truth, the truth which he has found will not be a doctrine; it will be a Person. The doctrine concerning this is no more than using words about it in the hope that the words may point to the reality. As we see it, truly Christian doctrine, if it could speak, would say like John the Baptist, "He must increase, but I must decrease." Then the least disciple in the Kingdom would be greater than the doctrine.

As faith is being displaced from Christ Himself to theology, something else may be happening at the same time. This also was to be seen in ancient Christianity. During apostolic times, an apostle's doctrine was received by the Christian community as inspired. Even then there were rival theologies, but after apostolic days the rivalry between theologies became heated, and the problem of distinguishing between them grew acute. In the great confusion which resulted it proved necessary that responsible authority should vouch for the theology. The story of those intricate passages in the history of the church cannot be told here; but in the course of time it came about that the authority which vouched for the theology was the church. That being so, the first movement of the believer's faith must be directed toward the church; then toward the doctrine concerning Christ which the church guaranteed; and finally, if the believer traveled that far in his faith, toward Christ Himself.

But the story still is not ended, for there were rival churches. This was true, of course, long before the Reformation; but after that crisis in Christian history the number of rival churches greatly increased, as even a child now knows. In consequence there is the inevitable third displacement of faith. One is not now called upon to have faith in the church as the Body of Christ, but rather in *the* church, that is to say in that church, whatever it be, to which he belongs.

Thus Christian faith becomes extraordinarily distorted in proportion as the believer responds to the claim that his own branch of Christianity is a unique repository of truth. The most active element in his faith may be a love of and a devotion to the points that distinguish him from other Christians. The one consuming loyalty in his religion, it may be, is his passion for one particular theory of the Bible, or the plan of salvation, or the return of our Lord, or the dispensations of history, or the sacraments, or any one sacrament, or the nature of ordination, or apostolic succession, or the polity (form of government) of the church, or any other distinguishing mark of the more than two hundred religious bodies found in the United States alone, to say nothing of other parts of the world.

Furthermore, it can hardly escape even the most casual observation that as a Christian's faith is displaced toward theology, or the church, or "my church," his open display of hostility and anxiety often increases. The facts involved are too well known to require more than the briefest reminder. On the international scale there have been the wars of religion. On the interdenominational scale there have been conflicts between established and dissenting churches, with the power of civil law and sword invoked against nonconforming Christians. Within a given religious body there have been inquisitions, heresy hunts, and the rack of mental or physical torture. As between liberal and conservative schools of thought or groups there have been invective, ridicule, and legal action. In individual lives of "defenders of the faith," there has sometimes been an incredible indifference to moral standards in pursuing some course of action which is justified by the needs of "the true faith." In short, all the phenomena of outcropping guilt which earlier we examined in the privacy of the clinic are also openly to be seen in the bosom of the church.

In the church, then, as outside it, two loves still struggle for mastery within the individual. Those two loves, as we have told, are Eros and Agape. Eros love, to say it again, is love whose motive is the enhancing of the self. Agape love is love whose motive is the enhancing of the beloved, and in the last analysis this Agape love comes to us from outside the human scene, seeking to liberate us from our hostility, our anxiety, and our guilt. Agape love which can liberate a man from these destroying demons within himself is offered in Jesus Christ. Faith arising from a man and directed toward Christ marks the turning point within that man; it is the beginning of his release.

But if the faith that is first offered to him and demanded of him is faith in something else than Christ Himself, whether it be in theology or in the church or in "my own part of the church," and is not first and foremost and always finally a faith in Christ Himself, then it can be said again as it was of old: He can there do no mighty works because of unbelief.

Thus the church, carrier of the story of the cross and offerer of eternal redemption, is itself and must always be under judgment. Were that all that is to be said we could only sigh and remark as men did shortly after the crucifixion, "We trusted that it had been he who should have redeemed Israel."

But that is *not* the end of the story. The Agape love from beyond man which shone forth in Christ did not end at Calvary. In the good providence of God there is in the universe still that which keeps that love active, forever invading man's life, again and again conquering man's own self-love as in St. Francis of Assisi and in those unknown disciples who live in every Caesar's household. In a word, a man has to reckon, even in the bosom of the church, with the Spirit of Christ as well as the Cross of Christ. To that we are now about to turn.

But here let us be certain that the chief point in all that we have been saying stands out. The cross is a word of God precisely to those who are under judgment and know that to be their case. That holds for the Christian who has displaced his love, as truly as it does for his brother; for each of them, it may be, is still worshipping the creation of his own hands, some theory in theology or politics, some structure of church or state which he has made and then deified. The moment when he knows that and "comes to himself" may be the moment when the miracle of redemption is about to break in on him and free him of his own chains.

In Wagner's "Tannhäuser" it is told with powerful symbolism in music as well as in words that a miracle must happen in the church as well as in the repentant sinner who seeks his salvation there. Tannhäuser has grown weary of the vortex of pleasure into which he plunged in the Hill of Venus and new love has come to him and he wishes to be absolved of his sin in order that he may be worthy of Elizabeth. He makes a pilgrimage to Rome and seeks absolution from the Pope himself. But he is told by the Pope that it is no more possible for him to be forgiven than for the staff in his hand to put forth leaves. Spurned by the Pope, he debates whether he shall return to the Hill of Venus and lose himself there again, and then the chant of a band of pilgrims is heard in the distance as they return from Rome. The cry of a messenger is heard shouting that a miracle has happened in the palace of the Pope. During the night the staff of the Pope has put forth fresh green leaves and he sends into every land to declare that this repentant sinner who sought pardon now has found it. The chorus of the pilgrims who sing this same good news ends with the triumphant words:

"The Lord Himself now thy bondage hath riven.
Go, enter in with the blest in His heaven."

All of which is to say that the miracle is not only in Tannhäuser, but also in the church whose dry, bejewelled wand of authority has itself come to life.

～ VII ～

THE SPIRIT OF CHRIST

THE INHERITANCE FROM JUDAISM

THE WRITERS of the New Testament inherited from Judaism two conceptions which are further refined in Christian thought, and eventually become of the greatest significance in the Christian experience and doctrine of redemption. One of these conceptions concerns the Spirit of God, the other the nature of man.[1]

Spirit of God. The Hebrew word *ruach* seems originally to have meant *wind,* that invisible power which we know by the same term, driving the chaff before it,[2] often accompanying a rain,[3] and clothed by imagination with wings.[4] It came also to mean *breath,* as though one thought of a lesser wind proceeding from the nostrils of a man.[5] But apparently even before it was used to signify breath it had already begun to be employed as a term by which one might refer to power coming forth from God, a power not seen but felt—God's *ruach* or Spirit. It could be regarded as capable of picking up a man bodily and carrying him away physically to some unknown destination and there dropping him.[6] Many times it is an evil spirit which comes upon a man from God, as with Saul.[7] It could represent an inrush of physical power as when the Spirit of God came mightily upon Samson, enabling him to break the cords that bound him as if they had been made of flax burnt by fire.[8] Apparently it could represent the power which caused states of frenzy and orgiastic excitement.[9]

But increasingly the term Spirit of God came to denote a power from God whose effect had some kind of ethical bearing. The Spirit enabled a man to be a judge of Israel,[10] or to deliver Israel from her oppressors.[11] Bezeleel was filled with the Spirit in order that he might become a master craftsman able to work cunningly, and for the glory of God, in his materials of brass and silver and gold.[12] But in the prophets the conception of the Spirit of God becomes a still more ethical one. The Spirit of God is especially prominent in the language of Isaiah and of Ezekiel. It was "the Lord God, and his Spirit," who sent Isaiah;[13] the Spirit of God was upon Isaiah to anoint him for the proclamation of his message;[14] thus the words which Isaiah speaks for God are an utterance which comes from beyond himself, and the expression "the word of God" becomes the general equivalent of the idea "the word of the Spirit of God."

In Ezekiel the Spirit is repeatedly spoken of as taking the prophet up,[15] lifting him up and taking him away,[16] falling upon him,[17] and the like; the Spirit enters into Ezekiel when the Lord speaks to him,[18] with the result that again the "word of the Lord" and the "word of the Spirit of the Lord" are virtually identical. Thus the older conception of the Spirit of God as a somewhat vague power rushing forth from God to produce physical effects has passed into a prophetic conception of the Spirit of God expressed in thought and through words, the words in turn being intended to produce moral results of a kind as revolutionary as when the spoken word raises a valley of dry bones and clothes them with garments of living flesh.[19]

The Nature of Man. If one would enter as fully as possible into Hebrew thought concerning the nature of man, perhaps his first task is to get rid of the Greek notion of man as body *and* soul. As we have seen earlier, Plato starts with the assumption that man is composed of body and soul; and thereafter he is never able to solve the problem of bringing the two into harmony; the soul can reach its true destination only when separated from the body. Much Christian thought has been built upon this Greek dichotomy in human nature, and it is impossible to say how great a portion of the popular doctrine of redemption has been discolored by the attempt to impose these Greek categories upon a Jewish-Christian stream of thought to which the Greek categories are almost completely alien.

The Hebrew saw man as a unity, not a dichotomy. God had made man out of the dust of the ground, had breathed into him the breath of life, and as a consequence man had become a living soul.[20] Man thus is not body and soul, but "animated body." His soul, or *nephesh,* is not something alien to his body, but instead is the animating principle of life in virtue of which he becomes a living creature in the first instance. Moreover, man's soul *(nephesh)* has come into him as a result of God's breathing into him. In other words, the Spirit of God has breathed the soul into man not as a separate entity apart from his body but as the life principle of that body.

The soul *(nephesh)* functions throughout the entire body. In Hebrew thought this can be stated in terms of either the whole or its parts. Viewing the body as a whole the Hebrew is able to make the statement that "the soul [*nephesh;* A.V. and A.S.V. 'life'] of the flesh is in the blood."[21] Or viewing the various parts of the body the Hebrew tended to see each part as the seat of some function of the soul. It must be understood, of course, that the Hebrew writers make no attempt at psychological precision in such matters, but with a fair degree of uniformity certain functions of the soul are thus localized.

For example, since the Spirit of God has breathed soul into man's nostrils, the nostrils both of man and of God serve an interesting twofold purpose. One is that the nostrils of man are an avenue by which the Spirit of God enters,[22] and it can be stated that "the spirit of God is in my nostrils."[23] But on the other hand the nostrils of God are not only the channel for His own breathing of soul into man, they are also the seat of the most tremendous anger on the part of God. The expressions at this point are graphic and powerful. The man who assumes the attitude of "holier than thou" is a smoke in the nostrils of God,[24] and that this is the equivalent of causing anger mighty enough to shake the earth is elsewhere evident,[25] for it is the nostrils of God which give forth the blast of His anger.[26]

Space will not permit presenting details of the functions served by the other parts of the body, for this material is very abundant and general statements must serve the purpose of showing what these are. "Heart" has so wide a range of meaning as to require two words, *lebh* and *lebabh;* the heart is the seat of what we call "mind," in such aspects as knowledge, thinking or reflection, and memory; it gathers up much that we mean by "will," also by "conscience," and "character"; and further is the seat of such feelings as sorrow, pain, joy, and gladness; from it come the inclinations toward good or evil. The reins, literally the kidneys, are the seat of passions or emotions the exact nature of which is obscure; it frequently is used as an expression parallel with "heart" and God is invited to try man's heart and reins; so a man's sincerity seems to be thought of as springing from his reins, and with the reins a man rejoices.

The term "bowels" denotes yet stronger shades of emotion, pre-dominantly emotions of a disturbing kind such as agitation,[27] anxiety,[28] fear,[29] and distress;[30] but it can also denote the strong and tender yearning of a woman toward a man.[31] Equally powerful emotions are denoted by the term "womb" (more properly the abdominal region), which refers to the yearnings of compassion or pity as felt by either a man[32] or a woman.[33] In short, what we now call consciousness spreads throughout all the body. The early Hebrew, of course, knew nothing of our modern term "the un-conscious," but it has several times been pointed out that they had its rough equivalent in their psychology; and it may be significant that the modern doctrine of the unconscious has been developed so largely by men of Jewish background.

Since the Hebrew regarded the soul of man as breathed into man by the Spirit of God, the Hebrew regarded man's primary obligation as being an obligation toward God. The tragedy of Judaism is that it could never fully clarify its own soul as to the nature of this obligation. Judaism contains two great streams of thought concerning this question. In one stream of thought it was held that a man's supreme obligation is to observe the Law, or Torah. Upon this foundation there arose the vast structure of Jewish law, the observing of which would bring a man into the only possible right relationship with God, and the neglect of which was cited to account for the misfortunes, the sufferings, and the disasters that befell Israel.

In the other stream of thought it was held that a man's supreme obligation was a responsiveness of "heart" to God. This theme comprises a great part of the prophetic utterances. But the prophets find the heart of man unresponsive to God. The theme with which Isaiah begins is a common one in the prophets; speaking for God, Isaiah says:

Hear, O heavens, and give ear, O earth: for the Lord hath spoken, I have nourished and brought up children, and they have rebelled against me. The ox knoweth his owner, and the ass his master's crib: but Israel doth not know, my people doth not consider. Ah sinful nation, a people laden with iniquity, a seed of evildoers, children that are corrupters: they have forsaken the Lord, they have provoked the Holy One of Israel unto anger.[34]

And finding man in rebellion against God, the prophet prevailingly sees no way to overcome the rebellion except to denounce the rebel. He is not able at any length to rise above his minor note of chiding complaint or thunderous invective against the sins of the people, whether in Jerusalem near at hand or in the East with its ferocious cruelty of warfare.

Furthermore, all that the prophet says of contemporary affairs is unquestionably true. That fact, together with the prophets' undoubted courage in speech, easily misleads the Christian of later times into supposing that the Hebrew prophets furnish the Christian his model way of confronting sin in personal and social life. But what seems not to be seen, in that view, is that the prophet typically does his work in an atmosphere of bristling hostility. Man is hostile to God—a rebel. God is hostile to man, pouring out wrath and woe. A great gulf is fixed between God and man, the prophet knowing no way to bridge it. Ranging himself as prophet on the side of God, the prophet pours forth his own hostility, assured, and rightly so, that he speaks in the name of God, yet not knowing how much of God he leaves out of his utterance. As has been said of a modern Christian prophet, so with many of the ancient prophetic deliverances: "He preaches the love of God with the deepest hatred." And preaching thus, the gulf is not crossed, nor the emotional underworld penetrated with something other than denunciation. Thus the heart is not won to God, but is only hardened against Him the more.

The Unconquered Underworld. The Jewish doctrine of the Spirit of God as the source of the human soul is unsurpassed in its simple majesty and suggestiveness. The Jewish psychology of man was realistic in its frank recognition of the emotional "underworld" of the human soul, stirring with its passions of love and hatred. But as we have just said, Jewish thought could visualize no adequate way by which the Spirit of God could invade and conquer the turbulent emotional underworld of the very soul which that Spirit had breathed into man. Had the Jew known a way by which the Spirit could invade and win the deep emotional underworld of human nature, his story as a race might have been far otherwise than it is.

For the Jew not only had a doctrine that man was in rebellion against God; he knew it as a fact of his own experience, and his sense of guilt was tremendous. As Rank observes, he not only had the sense of his own personal guilt, but had also internalized into himself as an individual a sense of participating in the collective guilt of the entire Jewish race.[35] But not having this insight, he did precisely the kind of thing which we have seen a man doing in modern times when he knows no adequate way to dispose of hostility and anxiety: he erected a barricade of ritual, sacrifice, and minute laws of conduct. We know from history that this "barricade" of Torah grew for centuries, based on the revealed Law of the Pentateuch, becoming larger and more minute in the Mishnah, and vaster still in the Talmud; the entire body of resulting law being regarded as revealed from heaven. We can also see this enormous body of Torah as a protection against an inward emotional problem which the religion was incapable of solving.

The inability to get a radical solution for the emotional problems involved in guilt is bound up with the conception of God, and that in two respects. First: as we have seen is the case in other religions, especially Greek religion, so in Judaism; when God is against man in his sin and does not go down with man into the hell of his suffering, the problem of guilt is insoluble. The second is like it; when it is not understood that the Spirit of God can perpetually penetrate to the depths of the emotional underworld and transform it, redemption tends to be externalized whether in Judaism or in Christianity. In Jewish thought there are glimpses of both these qualities in God. The Jewish prophet knew of a Suffering Servant, of Emmanuel, and of a new heart given by the Spirit. But these lay undeveloped in his theology, until they were taken up by the Christians. Of Christ as Suffering Servant who was Emmanuel,

"God with us" in human suffering, we have already spoken in the previous lecture. We may now turn to the Christian development of the understanding of the Spirit.

THE SPIRIT OF CHRIST

The history of *pneuma,* the Greek word for spirit, is very like that of the corresponding Hebrew word *ruach.* It meant wind, and breath, and was taken over to translate the Hebrew idea of *ruach* in reference to the Spirit of God. Readers of the Greek translation of the Old Testament thus were already familar with the expression "the *pneuma,* or Spirit of God."

The experience of the Spirit of God on the part of the early Christians is one of the most extraordinary aspects of the life of the primitive church. The description of the earliest days of the Christian community is given in the book of Acts, and evidently it is the intention of Luke to tell his readers that the birth of the Christian community was marked by an inrush of revolutionizing power which taxed the capacities of language to describe. There was "a sound . . . as of a rushing mighty wind,"[36] and "there appeared unto them cloven tongues like as of fire, and it sat upon each of them. And they were all filled with the Holy Ghost, and began to speak with other tongues, as the Spirit gave them utterance."[37]

By means of this and other dramatic accounts in the Acts we are being told that there is the most intimate association between two crucial events in the Christian revolutionizing of personality. In its simplest terms the association is this: when one genuinely believes in Christ he receives the Holy Spirit. When the matter was viewed from the angle of origins it could be held that the Spirit of God caused the faith to arise in a man—the faith is not of ourselves, "it is the gift of God."[38] Seen from that side, the resulting new life is a fresh creation by God; just as the soul or animating principle of life was originally breathed in by God, so the new life also is from that same source. But when viewed from the angle of the human being who experiences that faith, his faith results in the inflow of the Spirit.[39]

The nature of the revolution in personality wrought by the Spirit of God soon produced the gravest of questions. Again to put the case in its simplest terms, the question was whether the Spirit added gifts and powers which a man did not possess previously, or whether the Spirit changed and revolutionized what a man already had and was. Evidently both kinds of effects were experienced, and there is no sharp either/or between them; but, practically, which of the two should a man expect as a consequence of the coming of the Spirit?

Thus it became necessary very early in primitive Christianity to develop a doctrine of the Spirit as a means of guiding Christian experience. The Epistle to the Galatians probably is one of the oldest books of the New Testament, and in it one can see a re-markable doctrine of the Spirit already being clearly expressed. That doctrine of the Spirit has to do with changed character; that is, at the point where we first catch sight of a formulated doctrine of the Spirit of God, it is being taught by the apostle Paul that the primary function of the Spirit of God in human life is to reach down into the springs of human action and change the man himself. To the question of the way in which this change is wrought we are to return.

But here we are to observe an equally significant development which took place in the doctrine of the Spirit, that is, the "Spirit of Christ" becomes virtually indistinguishable from the "Spirit of God" or "Holy Spirit." In many instances, of course, the two terms ap-pear to be sharply distinct, but it seems evident that Christians were tending to identify the Spirit of Christ and the Spirit of God. It could be said, for example, that "God hath sent forth the Spirit of his Son into your hearts."[40] Again, in speaking of the ministrations of the Spirit, Paul can say that "the Lord is that Spirit."[41] Furthermore, the equating of the Spirit of Christ with the Spirit of God seems to be one of the purposes of the Gospel of John. Written probably as the doctrine of the Spirit was being clarified, the book lays great emphasis upon the promise of Christ that the Spirit would be sent to the believer; and it seems not too much to say that John wishes his readers to understand that the Spirit of God *is* the Spirit of Christ.

But the vast import of what was taking place is better seen if we observe some of the functions which the Spirit of Christ has in early Christian experience and in thought concerning that experience. At least six of these are worthy of note here. One is the appearance or realization of Christ, ordinarily to a believer who was in a moment of need or crisis. It has often been remarked that the entire tone of the accounts concerning Christ changes after the resurrection story has been completed. It is as if His going and coming were responsive, not to the ordinary natural laws, but to human need. Accounts of this nature in the latter portions of the Gospels are too well known to need repeating, but exactly similar experiences continue to be reported, as when Stephen in the hour of death seems to observe Christ; or "the Lord" appears to Paul in a time of danger.[42] Visions of Christ play a large part in the book of Revelation, and the "angel of the Lord" similarly is a frequent figure in the earliest accounts of the church. The fact that many of these are "visions" is exactly the point; in moments of crisis the believer frequently not only felt that he was not alone, but reported experiencing the presence of the risen Christ.

These visionary states give place to other experiences and conceptions which begin to signify that Christ is always present with the believer in one or another respect, not as a temporary vision but as an abiding presence. There is, for example, the idea of "membership," signifying that the believer in some sense is a part of Christ and that Christ in turn is the head of the body whose members are the believers. A very similar idea is expressed by the thought of "indwelling"—when one believes in Christ, loves Him and obeys His commandments, Christ abides in the believer and the believer abides in Christ, after the similitude of vine and branches.

The meaning of membership and indwelling is brought to another kind of focus by the thought that the believer may have in him "the mind of Christ"; and when this is so, one of the decisive aspects of the mind of Christ comes to characterize the believer also, that is, the believer then breaks out of his own Eros love with his protections of his own dignity and prestige, and gives himself in Agape love toward others, thereby sharing in the exaltation that has come to Christ Himself.[43]

Thus it is but a step more to regard Christ Himself as either being or embodying the creative principle in the universe. It is the Logos by whom all things were made.[44] Paul has a similar view: "By him were all things created, that are in heaven, and that are in earth, visible and invisible, whether they be thrones, or dominions, or principalities, or powers: all things were created by him, and for him: and he is before all things, and by him all things consist."[45] We shall probably miss the force of such thought unless we see it as possibly being concerned chiefly with the creation of new selves or personalities within the new relationship. As Paul elsewhere puts it, "For in Christ Jesus neither circumcision availeth any thing, nor uncircumcision, but a new creation."[46] In a striking parallel to this passage Paul also writes, "For in Christ

Jesus neither circumcision availeth anything nor uncircumcision, but faith which worketh through love."[47] Here faith "energizing" through love may be taken as the manward side of God's creative act.

The Spirit of Christ also fulfills the function of judgment. But it is no longer the kind of judgment with which Hebrew prophecy abounds. It is no longer the Deity standing over against man at a vast distance from him, and denouncing him. It is the Spirit of that same Deity internalized within the believer. This internalized Spirit provides a new standard for a new kind of judgment. What that is, is illustrated in Jesus' parable of the Last Judgment where the final test of a man's standing in the eyes of the King is not his observance of a code of law but rather is his ability to see the simple needs of his fellow man as Christ saw them, and to meet those needs by acts of a genuine outgoing love as Christ Himself met them.[48] In that same vein Paul can sum up a long line of abstract reasoning by saying, "If any man have not the Spirit of Christ, he is none of his."[49] And the effects of that Spirit are felt as liberty,[50] a release *from* the negatives of religion, and a release *into* the unlimited possibilities of a personality set free by Christ.

If now the change that has come into the concept "Spirit of God" can be viewed as a whole it is apparent that the concept has been filled with new meaning because the experience itself has moved out into new depths. The Spirit of God is no longer a somewhat vague power, but has now become intensely personalized. The Spirit of God did not lack personality throughout all of the Old Testament; yet the character of that personality is not fully revealed there. *The Spirit of God is now a Person, having the same character or mind as Christ, and able everywhere in any time to produce the same effects as Christ did in human personality.*

Thus God goes down into the hell which man has made, not

only by the Cross of Christ, but also by the Spirit of Christ. This personalized Spirit is capable of penetrating into the emotional "underworld" and transforming it. What that emotional underworld is in New Testament thought may be better seen by examining the view of human nature which is there expressed.

THE NATURE OF MAN

In the New Testament, as in Hebrew thought, man is a unity, not a dichotomy. The Greek term *psyche* means soul just as the Hebrew term *nephesh* does, and seldom if ever in the New Testament do we encounter the classic Greek notion that man is body *and* soul. It is well to recognize that the word "soul" covers a wide range of meaning and that the usage is perplexing in some respects.[51] But prevailingly, if not always, soul means life, and many of the passages where the word is used not only gain greater force but probably are nearer to the thought of the writer if *psyche* is translated *life*. Thus in the famous saying of Jesus, "What shall it profit a man, if he shall gain the whole world, and lose his own soul?" the context shows that the edge of the statement points to what happens in a man's *life* here and now.[52] Or, to approach what is essentially the same question from a different angle, salvation is of the entire personality, in New Testament thought, and not of some segment of that personality; so much so that repeatedly no more is said than that *"you"* shall be saved, which is simply to say that the object of redemption is the entire man.

This is more clearly seen in Pauline thought than elsewhere in the New Testament, as far as a formal psychology is concerned, for Paul probably comes nearer than any other Biblical writer to presenting a complete psychology of man. Even in his writings a given term may vary in meaning, enough so to make precise definitions of his terms hazardous; but for all that, his conception of man can be seen in its general outlines.

With Paul, redemption is *redemption of the body*. The phrase itself is his[53] and in order to grasp his conception of redemption, one must see what a "Pauline man" is. Obviously Paul is not writing a systematic, scientific treatise on man, and the dry exactness which goes into that kind of literature is not to be found in Paul. Moreover, one function, such as thinking, may be described under two or more terms. But even within such limitations it is possible to see that Paul considers man from three points of view. If those can be distinguished without falling into scholastic hair-splitting, much confusion as to Paul's meaning can be avoided and his daring conception of redemption can stand out the more clearly. In brief, Paul views man sometimes as a whole, sometimes by parts of the whole, and sometimes as the scene of conflict. The latter subject will be considered in the next lecture. The drawing on the next page may serve to illustrate the three conceptions.

The Whole. When Paul views man as a whole he may use either the term body or the term soul. The body is the entire organism, which is a unity and which has hands, feet, ears, eyes, etc. When the same organism is thought of as a creature having life, it is "soul." This is the sense in which Paul most frequently uses the word soul—to indicate life, as contrasted with non-life, or with dying.[54] Paul sometimes uses the term in a way which suggests that he is thinking primarily of a living creature as a responsible being.[55]

Elsewhere in the New Testament "soul" is frequently used in enumerations, indicating such and such a number of individual persons; Paul uses the word in this sense probably but twice.[56] Other New Testament writers often use "soul" to indicate a living being

THE PAULINE MAN

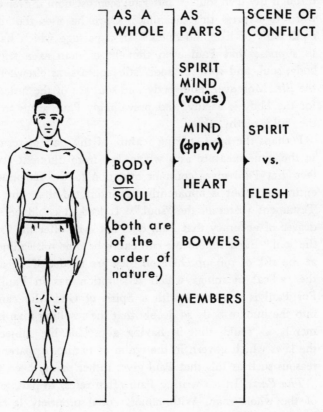

AS A WHOLE	AS PARTS	SCENE OF CONFLICT
	SPIRIT MIND (voûs)	
BODY OR SOUL (both are of the order of nature)	MIND (φpnv)	SPIRIT vs. FLESH
	HEART	
	BOWELS	
	MEMBERS	

capable of strong feelings, as in the saying "a sword shall pierce through thy own soul";[57] but Paul seems seldom if ever to need this word to express this meaning.[58] Once he uses the term as the equivalent of likemindedness.[59] In a passage which has led some to suppose that Paul even thought of man as a trichotomy of body, soul, and spirit,[60] "soul" still appears, as elsewhere, to mean the *life*. Moreover, both body and soul are of the order of nature, for the body is earthy, and prevailingly Paul seems to mean that the soul is earthy, also.

Perhaps the most striking feature of this pair of terms referring to the same creature as a whole, but from different angles, is the fact that Paul gives constant attention to the redemption of the entire man, but is apparently less interested than any other New Testament writer in the "soul."[61] Indeed, it could be said with a degree of accuracy that Paul does not even offer the "salvation of the soul." Such statements can easily become misleading, but even at the risk of misapprehension they are needed if we are to sense the radical meanings which redemption has in Paul's thought. For Paul is concerned with a Spirit of God who can penetrate into the human body so deeply that the resulting man is no longer merely a "soul," that is, having a psychic life subject solely to the laws which govern in the realm of nature. Apparently it is for reasons such as this that Paul gives rather scanty heed to the soul.

The Parts. In his writing Paul often refers to parts or functions of the whole man. With almost equal propriety it can be said that these are functions of either the body or the soul. Among the more notable of these terms for parts or functions of the whole man are mind, diaphragm, heart, bowels, and members.

For "mind" Paul uses two words, *nous* which is the more common, and *phren*. *Nous* is man's intellect; it corresponds roughly with what is meant by "reason" in the Renaissance, and in philosophical writing. It is that in man which renders him capable of perceiving, thinking, reasoning, understanding, judging, and willing. *Nous* functions in at least five ways. One, which is specifically the activity of *nous (noeo)*, represents a man's ability to reason concerning a matter, to come to understand it, or to pass judgment regarding it. The result of this activity is his "thoughts" *(noemata)*. Three other kinds of mental activity presumably are functions of the *nous,* at least in part. One is to know intuitively *(oida),* with the suggestion that we know some things as if we had seen them with the eyes. Another is to know by experience *(ginosko),* while the third is to know *thoroughly* by experience *(epiginosko).* Furthermore, the will *(thelema),* or the act of willing *(thelein),* is a function of the mind.[62]

By virtue of having a mind *(nous),* man has a spiritual capacity. That is to say, he can reason concerning God *(noeo);*[63] can intuitively apprehend God *(oida);*[64] can know God in experience *(ginosko);*[65] or better still can have so intimate and deep an experiential knowledge of God *(epignosis)*[66] as to be superior to a merely rational knowledge of Him. But these are latent capacities, and until they are quickened, the thoughts of man's mind *(noemata)* may be blinded;[67] or even the mind *(nous)* itself is corrupt.[68]

The second word for mind, *phren,* literally means midriff or diaphragm. Perhaps the upper part of the trunk of the body is meant. Whereas *nous* is the more intellectual and rational mind, *phren* seems to suggest a kind of thinking where feeling and habit are prominent. With the *phren* one may be childish or hold malice.[69] With this kind of thinking *(phroneo)* one passes opinion or judgment upon himself or others;[70] with the thoughts of the *phren (phronema)* one is minded toward the flesh or toward the Spirit.[71]

The next part of the body to be considered in Paul's writing is the heart. Heart *(kardia)* has almost as varied a usage as it does in our common speech. It seems generally to connote some activity or experience in which the passions, the desires, the appetites, the affections, or in a word the feelings and emotions, are involved. In Paul, the heart is the source from which lust flows.[72] In consequence, bodies are dishonored, affections are vile, and there are unnatural relations between men and men, and between women and women. Yet in the heart the works of the law are written,[73] so much that in being a natural law unto oneself, man is that far acknowledging the valid claim of the law of God upon his own conscience. Thus the heart as Paul uses the term is the spring from which *by nature* there comes both what God condemns and something at least of what God requires.

Faith in Christ springs from the heart. True belief in Him comes from the heart.[74] Turning the matter the other way around, the test of the sincerity of faith is whether it comes from the heart. Just as the only true circumcision is that of the heart,[75] and the only acceptable obedience is that which comes from the heart,[76] so the faith that justifies the believer and opens him to transforming grace, is faith from the heart.[77] The point is important, not only for an understanding of Paul, but in ascertaining the nature of faith itself. By insisting that saving faith is from the heart it is significant that the saving quality in faith is not the giving of credence to propositions concerning Christ, but is a change of the affections, the initial stages of a new, redeeming love to the Lord of life.

By persons who spoke Greek, as with those who used Hebrew, the term "bowels" *(splangchna)* was identified with powerful emotions which are physically felt in the viscera, or generally in the nether part of the body trunk. Greek poets associated the viscera both with negative emotions such as anger and anxiety, and with the positive emotions such as affection and pity. Interest-ingly, the *splangchna* indicated a man's true nature. By the time of the Christian era the word seems to have been restricted to positive emotions, such as compassion and the like. It probably is significant in this connection that Greek and Roman augurs inspected the viscera of a sacrificial victim as a way of foretelling the future. A sort of priestly "science" grew up around this practice, and a devout person could speak of dedicating his viscera to Jupiter.

When Paul uses the term *splangchna,* as he frequently does,[78] his language unfortunately cannot be literally translated into English without diverting modern readers from the immense vigor of what he is saying, and attempted equivalents such as "tender mercies" are rather insipid. He always uses the word in a context where a tender but exceedingly deep and moving emotion is felt or described, and, perhaps most significant of all, he never uses this word for profound tenderness except in connection with the emotions of Christ or the Christian believer. This seems to imply that the tenderest affections of which human nature is capable can be quickened only in those whose whole being is under transformation in response to the unutterable love of Christ; and even then these tenderest affections need yet further enlarging, like a straitened house which is too narrow for the Spirit of Christ to dwell in.[79]

Paul also attaches much importance to the "members of the body." These members of the body are its "parts," such as head, ears, eyes, nose, hands, feet, "uncomely parts," and so forth.[80] The members do not have the same "office," yet the body is one.[81] Thus the idea "members" represents on one hand the unity of the body, and on the other hand represents any of the functions exercised by the entire personality as it seeks its goals. So the acts performed or the habitual bent of the desires are "members" of the body, such as fornication, uncleanness, inordinate affections, concupiscence, and covetousness.[82]

Furthermore, there is a "law" working in man's members,[83] a "law" which is contrary to the "law of the Spirit"; this "law" represents the "motions of sin," the emotional strivings[84] of Eros self-love as a man pampers himself in meat and drink, dreams of sexual conquests wherever his fancy roams and achieves such as he can; seethes in hatred, wrath, and envy; devotes himself to unrewarding loyalties, is continually splitting the groups of which he is a member, and on occasion is a killer whether by act or word.[85] That is to say, the "members" stand for every function of the body by which man engages in living, functions by which it is natural for him to hew toward his own instinctive goals and let the chips fall where they will in home, church, or state. The "members" are self-protecting, self-gratifying, self-enhancing Eros love in action in the raw. Their "law" is the law of self-expression when the self has not yet begun to be touched by grace.

THE TRANSFORMING SPIRIT

In the Pauline conception of redemption the Spirit of God permeates the entire body. As has been observed, the Spirit of God becomes a personalized reality in experience, and a personalized concept in thought, generally equivalent to the Spirit of Christ. The core of the matter is that this personalized Spirit goes down into the human body until the Spirit of Christ has wrought, or begins to work, the most radical revolution of which the body is capable. Once Paul uses the term "the love of the Spirit": "I beseech you, brethren, by our Lord Jesus Christ, and by the love of the Spirit,"[86] where not only does "the Lord Jesus Christ" parallel "the Spirit" and perhaps equate with it, but where also the love borne by the Spirit to man is prominent. The love borne by the Spirit of Christ into the hearts of men may or may not be the exact idea here, but at least it is true that throughout the entire body of Pauline writing this idea is put forward in a great multiplicity of shadings and expressions. The love of the Spirit transforms the believer.

The initial entry of the Spirit into man may be described in either of two ways. Apparently the more common conception in Paul is that man hears the gospel of Christ,[87] so that the entry of the Spirit is into the mind either as *nous*,[88] or as *phren*,[89] and as we have said, the response of true faith is from the heart. In virtue of this conception Paul attributes the greatest significance to preaching the gospel, so that man may hear and believe.[90]

Again Paul *may* mean that the Spirit of God comes into man's spirit. It is difficult to say with certainty whether Paul thinks of man as having, or being, spirit at all until man has begun to respond to God's Spirit. Two or three times he refers to the spirit of a man in a context which suggests a psychological entity,[91] but the interpretation even here is doubtful, and he may mean no more than some characteristic quality or bent. Again there is some ground for asserting that in Paul's thought the soul, which is of the order of nature, becomes a spirit only when the Spirit quickens a man and when in consequence faith has begun.[92]

But in any event, whether the ingress of the Spirit is into man's spirit or whether, as seems more clearly expressed, it is into the mind, *the Spirit is conceived in Paul as transforming both the body as a whole and its constituent parts.*

Regarding the body as a whole, it must not fail to be observed that when Paul has completed what is commonly called the doctrinal part of the Epistle to the Romans, he prefaces the so-called ethical section by an injunction which sums up the response of man to the redeeming love of God by saying: "I beseech you therefore, brethren, by the mercies of God, that ye present your bodies a living sacrifice, holy, acceptable unto God, which is your reasonable service."[93] We have already called attention to the view in Paul that redemption itself is redemption of the body. Christ is to be magnified in the believer's body.[94]

This conception of redemption is made the more powerful when it is further seen that Paul regards the "natural body" as transformed into a "spiritual body" at the resurrection of believers who have undergone physical death.[95] He draws a startling contrast between two kinds of body; the one is the *soma psychikon* (natural body), that is, the body which is of the order of nature, having had *psyche* or animal life breathed into it; the other, the *soma pneumatikon* (spiritual body), the transformed, fully redeemed, resurrected body which has had the Spirit of God breathed into it. This conception of a "spiritual body" is full of the greatest difficulty for modern minds, but that fact need not for one moment deter us from regarding Paul's thought of the redeemed body as one of the most daring conceptions of the entire New Testament. For in this conception the believer's body-soul is metamorphosed finally and eternally into a body-spirit.[96]

But the changes in the body which are wrought by Spirit are not, in Paul, restricted to the future. On the contrary, they commence as soon as faith begins. For with the coming of the Spirit there begins a transformation of the very same parts of the body which comprise the whole body. The mind, or *nous,* is "renewed" with transforming effect upon the entire body.[97] The *phren,* or habitual inclinations, literally the diaphragm, is no longer bent toward "the flesh," but toward the things of the Spirit.[98]

As to those parts of the body which more distinctively represent feelings and emotions, the descriptions of the changes wrought are varied. Much is said of the effects of the Spirit in the heart. God sends the Spirit of His Son into the heart;[99] the result is that Christ dwells in the heart;[100] in the heart is given the light of the knowledge of the glory of God in the face of Jesus Christ;[101] the love of God is shed abroad in the heart because the Spirit has entered it;[102] the peace of God rules in the heart;[103] the eyes of the heart are enlightened;[104] and all these and other results of such a kind are "earnests" of the Spirit in the heart, that is, down payments to prove what the Spirit is capable of doing in the heart and is pledged still to do in the future.[105]

And if Paul had used the term "the unconscious" he probably would have said that the Spirit goes down even into that abyss of a man's nature to transform it also. He did not have that term but unmistakably he had its equivalent under other symbols, especially the heart, the *splangchna*, and the "members." For not only is the love of God shed abroad in the heart by the Spirit, but in the same Spirit the "members" begin to yield to other ends— to "righteousness" instead of "unrighteousness";[106] that is to say, the entire personality begins now to function in quest of new goals in living.

Then two other results of greatest consequence begin to take place. The first is that the believer himself now becomes a "member" of Christ,[107] signifying that one who has believed "into Christ" commences now to be a functioning part of "the body of Christ" of which we are yet to speak. For the moment it is enough to say that the lone soul of the animal creation has become part of something both human and divine, greater and stronger than himself.

And as a second consequence the violent emotions aroused by the dangers, frustrations, and insecurities of living begin to subside, giving place to the sway of *splangchna*, those powerful but tender emotions of one who is "in the Lord," who is moved by emotions akin to His,[108] and both finds and arouses similar emotions in other believers.[109] The profound conquest of the more violent emotions in the life of Jesus Christ, that Lord who *is* the Spirit, is remarkably illustrated in Matthew. The "woes" there uttered represent, we may believe, the anger arising against the Pharisees after months of frustration at their hands. But scarcely are they ended before one hears the words of deep yearning: "O Jerusalem, Jerusalem, thou that killest the prophets, and stonest them which are sent unto thee, how often would I have gathered thy children together . . ."[110] So has Agape love triumphed over frustration and anger; and so is it to be, Paul is saying, with the one who is "in Christ." Agape can invade even the unconscious, and win.[111]

THE NEW LIFE

Jakob Boehme, who did not care too much about formal theology but did know God by having met Him, wrote,

> I can neither write nor tell of what sort of Exaltation the triumphing in the Spirit is. It can be compared with nought, but that when in the midst of death life is born, and it is like the resurrection of the dead.[112]

So said John, Paul, and others who had met God in Christ, each in his own manner of speaking. For they give us the two classic summary descriptions of what takes place within one who responds to Christ by faith, and in whom the resulting new life begins. Both descriptions, be it observed, are cast in terms of *life,* and not in legalisms whether of heavenly or earthly courts.

For John, the decisive change means that one is born again. In the fourth Gospel, Christ is life coming into the scene of death. The man who believes forsakes the realm of death and darkness, enters into life and light. John is not so much concerned with explaining his thesis, as he is with stating it as a Gospel and *illustrating* how life and light come to those who believe in Christ. To believe was to be reborn. If a learned man, hearing, was left pondering literal-mindedly whether rebirth meant entering again into the mother's womb and beginning thence anew, John is content to leave this teacher of religion to struggle with the theology and the biology of the new life. In due time redeeming truth—which with John is a Person, not an abstraction—[113] might strike home even to a doctor of religious law.

For Paul the decisive change which comes with the first motions of true faith in Christ is death and resurrection, not futuristically but here and now. He knows of a resurrection in the future, well enough; but for Paul the resurrection of the body begins *now*, just as with John eternal life begins now.

The death and resurrection of Jesus was at the very heart of Paul's gospel,[114] and the believer shared in both the death and the resurrection. And in the last analysis, as must be said again, the death and resurrection of the believer in the present are not legalisms but vitalisms—the dying of an "old man," and the rising of a "new man" who henceforth is to "walk in newness of life,"[115] of which inward things baptism was his outward symbol.[116]

THE SPIRIT AS PERSON

Christianity signifies not only that God comes into man's plight and stands beside him as "we," but also that God by His Spirit, which is the Spirit of Christ, goes down by the consent of a man's faith into the Augean stable of human personality itself and begins the transformation of that personality, not merely by way of superficially altering the articles of a credal faith, but by radically changing and redirecting the springs of human action which are in the realm of feeling and emotion.

In any attempt to reckon with what is meant by the Spirit of God, we thus are still in the realm of personality as surely as with the earthly Christ. No less than when man confronted Him in the flesh, it is a matter still of relationship, the relationship between a man and God as He is manifested in Christ.

✠ VIII ➤

THE BODY OF CHRIST

THE FELLOWSHIP OF THE SPIRIT

Identification and Individuality. At an earlier stage of the thought we are pursuing in these lectures, attention was drawn to two needs which must be met if the human being is to thrive. One is the need for identification with something greater and stronger than oneself; the other, the need for individuality, that is, the right to become a self-governing person.

It was pointed out that both these needs begin to exist from the hour of birth. It has further been shown repeatedly and in many ways, that if either of these is sought at the neglect of the other, a stalemate of human development results. It has been shown too, now, that Christianity proposes a unique way of meeting both these needs of human nature by means of faith in Christ. Among other things, faith in Christ *is* identification with Christ; and as a consequence of genuine faith, genuine freedom of personality begins to develop. This much we have presented at some length.

But now it is to be seen, further, that by one of the most remarkable developments of thought in the New Testament, identification with Christ comes to mean *also* identification with and participation in a social organism of a unique kind. This organism is the church, and the church becomes the *Body of Christ.*

The idea of the church as the Body of Christ gives Christianity one of the most profound conceptions of society ever expressed. Any attempt at a full consideration of it lies beyond the scope of these lectures. But inasmuch as our theme has to do with guilt and redemption, it can be said at once that in this New Testament conception, the church as the Body of Christ is a society within whose relationships the divine pledge of redemption from guilt is meant to be realized. Thus the New Testament conception of redemption is kept within the area of relationships.

Koinonia. The redemptive character of those relationships is not fully brought out by Agape, important as that kind of love is in effecting the breakout from self-destroying Eros love. When Agape love exists between persons, they are in what the New Testament knows as *koinonia,* which is a communion, a fellowship, a sharing. It exists between believers and God, so much so that in the trine benediction the peculiar gift of the Spirit is fellowship. It exists between believers, and characterizes their relationships as being between persons who are equals before God, and who build each other up ("edify") in any needed way, whether by bread when bread is needed, or by a mutual sharing of strength, courage, spiritual insight, or spiritual triumph.

Fellowship *(koinonia)* in the Body of Christ is symbolized in the communion of the Lord's Table. How easily the reality behind this symbol is violated and dragged back to the plane of fleshly motive, is nowhere more strikingly shown than in the fact that the Lord's Supper has become a token of spiritual exclusiveness whereby one group of believers shut themselves in and shut others out from communion. This extraordinary state of things within Christianity has been encouraged by at least three kinds of abstractions. Mention of these may serve not only to show how easily the reality of fellowship is violated as respects this symbol of it, but, more important, it will show that *the same kind of guilt in the church which violates the symbolic communion also renders it more difficult for the Body of Christ* to become the body of human relationships within which genuine redemption from guilt can be achieved.

Abstractions. Christianity has tended to make just such abstractions as we are talking of, when it constructs a theology of redemption. It has lifted out relatively small pieces of the whole meaning of redemption, made these into systems, and then trusted the system of doctrine as if *it* had saving grace. In so doing it seems to have overlooked a fact which the New Testament makes perfectly plain. The doctrine of redemption was presented piecemeal to Christians in churches, Christians who did not yet know how their own continuing guilt, hostility, and anxiety could be put with utter confidence in the hands of the same God who had already begun to redeem them. Since the original basis for a Christian doctrine of redemption from guilt comes to us in such a setting, it is reasonable to hold that its most effective continuing use will be in a similar setting, namely, within a body of believers who continue to struggle with their own guilt.

Again, Christianity has tended to create an abstraction which is called ecclesiology, the supposed science of the church. The issues attacked in this branch of Christian thought have ordinarily been controversial, since the questions which proved to be of greatest interest were those touching the government of the church, which means that this science represents the concern of the cleric to get and hold authority over his fellow Christians. Continuing Eros self-love in the Christian has seldom been more clearly shown than in the degree to which each body of Christians is able to prove to its own satisfaction that one's own branch of the church exhibits the one divinely sanctioned form of church government. But once more it might have been observed, had we had eyes open to see it, that the New Testament portrays to us a church, or churches if such be one's preference for expressing it, consisting of sinful persons with continuing self-assertion, continuing devices for gaining prestige, and a continuing readiness to destroy the very organism which, as the Body of Christ, was seeking to bring Agape love into their living. Fortunately the twentieth century sees an attempt to rediscover the meaning of the church, but unhappily this attempt has thus far foundered repeatedly on the rock of clerical self-assurance which, again, may be but another symptom of our own guilt.

Yet again, Christianity has tended to rear an abstract doctrine of ethics. The result has been a creature for textbooks, a thing so dull ordinarily that few can be persuaded to study it, and so idle that when they do study it, they have little to show for their pains except divisive resolutions about unreal issues. But ethics, as the New Testament so plainly shows, has to do with decisions for action in the face of practical issues which confront the persons concerned, issues moreover which they are called upon to settle then and there as members of the Body of Christ, and cannot settle before the issues arise.

We are now to consider a few of the ways by which the theology and the Christian ethic are not abstractions from life to be put in a book, but strong meat for building up the relationships within the Christian society so that these may become truly redemptive.

THE SMITHS

In order to avoid some of the very abstractions of which we have just been speaking, it may prove profitable to take an actual case. The story of the Smith family would require a book itself, but the fragments of its life told here will illustrate in part, although only in part, certain elements in redemption from guilt which need to be still further considered from the standpoint of Christianity.

In the Smith family the four persons with whom we are chiefly concerned are the father, Arthur Smith; Dora, who is his second wife; and their two children, Dorothy age nineteen and Alex now about seventeen. All are members of a church served by the Reverend W. J. D. Arthur Smith's mother appears occasionally in the family and is described as a suspicious, dominating woman whose character is dubious, and who often interferes in the Smiths' affairs. Arthur's father and mother separated when he was quite young and he describes his childhood as being decidedly unhappy. By Arthur's first marriage there were two children, but the marriage ended in divorce and the children went with the mother, so they do not enter this account any further. Arthur was a Roman Catholic until his second marriage, when he became a Protestant. Then, with his wife, he entered the membership of Mr. D's church, where he soon became an officer.

At the depth of the economic depression Smith became despondent. Missing him one day, his wife, Dora, went to the basement where she discovered that he had cut his throat and was standing there, razor in hand, bleeding profusely. He was rushed to the hospital, where he recovered, and returned to his home and later found work again.

When Mr. D became pastor of the Smith family he soon observed that Alex, then about fourteen years of age, frequently grew agitated during the church service. Some of the officers of the church remarked to Mr. D that they believed Alex was losing his mind. One night Alex came to the minister's house, asked for the minister and his wife, and told them his story. In this particular church the sacrament of the Lord's Supper was observed monthly, and it was the custom of the church to present an offering on that Sunday for charitable purposes. Alex told that when he was about eight years of age he had no spending money, his father was out of work, and the sight of the money near the Communion table was too much for him. As the members of the congregation went forward to kneel and to receive the Communion and then to remain for a few moments in meditation with eyes closed, Alex, kneeling with them, would take money from the plate.

He had continued this practice for some two years, but he grew increasingly remorseful. He described times when he would go with his father to a meeting of a board of church officers and would hear the officers asking what could have become of the money put in the Communion offering. One would say, "I know that a five dollar bill was put in the offering last Sunday, but when we counted the money there was no five dollar bill there." At such a time, Alex said, he would almost spring to his feet and admit his guilt, but fear held him back. Often during the church service, he said, he would grow so excited that he could scarcely hold himself in his seat. He could not tell his parents, for he said, "They would beat me to death." Now he could bear it no longer, and asked the minister, "What can I do to make it right?"

Mr. D asked Alex, "How much do you owe?" The boy replied, "It's $40.75. But now I haven't got but a dollar. I have to stay in school and can't get a job. Father can't give me but a wee little allowance, and I don't see any way in the world to pay it back until I can get a job."

Now it chanced that the church was in arrears with Mr. D's salary by the amount of $40.00. So it was arranged that Alex would owe the money to Mr. D and that the latter should cancel the obligation which the church owed him. Mr. D related to the treasurer of the church simply that a certain member of the congregation had turned over to him $40.00, or its equivalent, but did not bring Alex's name into the account in any manner.

Then the boy wished to know whether he could be forgiven. The minister told him stories of Christ and forgiveness, and assured him that God forgives all those who ask Him to do so. Peace seemed to return to the boy; he was no longer so restless during the church service, and many times he has told Mr. D that the sense of guilt and the worry have gone completely.

But a feeling of strain still pervaded the Smith household. The father continued to domineer over his children. Mr. Smith's birthday was approaching. He suggested to his wife that he wished a hat as a birthday present, but his birthday came and Dora had forgotten to buy the hat. In the house, however, there was a woman rooming with the family, and on the evening of the birthday she presented Arthur Smith with the hat which he had desired. He upbraided his wife for her forgetfulness, had much to say about being shut out of the family circle where no one remembered him, and continued to brood over the incident for a long while. One evening when Mr. D returned home he found Alex lying on the couch in the minister's house, weeping and incoherent. Finally Alex was able to tell the minister that Arthur Smith had made violent scenes at home, driving Alex from the house, beating the daughter, and locking himself in his room where he refused to see anyone.

Uncertain as to the proper course of action the family asked the minister to call a doctor and the latter advised that Arthur be placed in a psychopathic ward of a hospital, since there was danger that he might injure himself or others. During detention in the hospital members of the family visited Smith frequently, seeking to reassure him of his place in their affections. Upon his release he again returned to work and has resumed an apparently normal course of life, including his duties in the church.

As time has passed Mr. D, sensing the continuing tension in the family, has sought in many ways to bring the members of the family into natural associations both in work and in play. The mother was made church treasurer and Alex was appointed her assistant. Members of the family were put on the same church committees, and paired together in games played at social gatherings. In his preaching Mr. D has often taken occasion to treat some problem in a manner which he hoped would suggest to the Smiths the resources that are in Christianity.

Among the many issues still confronting the various members of this family, is one which Alex still has to solve, and that is the question of his career. He desires to be a medical missionary, but the father contends that the education for this career is too expensive and too long and constantly urges Alex to become a bookkeeper since the father feels that the pay is good and the training is not so long. But Alex is determined to become a medical missionary, feeling certain that this is the will of God for him.

As one considers the situation confronted by each member of this family he is quickly aware of the many angles from which the problems of any one of the four could be regarded. However, instead of approaching the matter in this fashion, we shall have the Smiths in the background of thought as we turn to certain great issues involving guilt and redemption, as these are approached in the New Testament.

The Continuing Conflict

On one hand the New Testament writers insist that God through Christ or through the Spirit can go down to the very roots of a human being and transform the self completely. But on the other hand these same writers recognize with entire frankness that, as a matter of fact, a Christian believer is *not* completely transformed. On the contrary, he continues to be a scene of conflict.

The nature of the conflict is variously described in the New Testament, but two conceptions of it stand out. For John there is conflict in the universe itself between light and darkness. But the conflict is personalized, that is, the Word, Logos, of God, Jesus

Christ who "became flesh, and dwelt among us," *is* the light; as John puts it, the life is the light of men. Men love darkness rather than light; and the emphasis is upon their *love* of darkness. A man may remove forever from the plane of darkness into that of light by receiving Christ—believing in Him, loving Him. Such are given power—or, better, the right—to become the sons of God. When they become sons of God, both the nature and the object of their love change.

The teaching of John as regards conflict in the believer *after* he has become a believer, will bear divergent interpretations. Some hold that John's writings can be understood only in terms of an absolute ideal. A man is either in Christ, or not in Christ. He who is born of God does not and cannot go on sinning.[1] If he is in Christ he is "in the light"; if not in Christ, he is "in darkness." There are no shadings between perfect light and complete darkness. In this view it is said that John knows nothing, or at least says nothing, regarding continuing conflict in the believer. If this view be the most dependable interpretation, John has nothing for the man who believes he has believed, and who yet continues to struggle with his own sin. Such a man is not yet a true believer, *i. e.,* his Agape love toward Christ is not perfect.

Others, however, hold that certain sayings of John *do* recognize conflict as continuing in the believer. John seems to say unmistakably that no believer is free from sin; one who maintains he is free from sin deceives himself and makes God a liar.[2] If this view of the meaning of the passage in its setting is correct, this is but to say that the believer, although now in the light, continues to manifest works of darkness. He still is a scene of conflict, for he is not yet "made perfect in love."[3] Thus, finally, in either view, John gives the highest significance to the development of love (Agape) as an index to a man's progress or decline as a child of God.

For Paul the conflict is between flesh and Spirit. This is not the same as the Platonic conflict between body and soul, for in Paul ordinarily flesh is not the equivalent of body, nor is the body as such evil, and as has already been shown, soul is not the same as spirit in Paul. The conflict between flesh and Spirit is a conflict between two principles contending for mastery of the believer's body and therefore of all his thought, feeling, and action.

Flesh commonly represents either or both of two ideas. One is that man as body or soul is a part of nature, and as such seeks his own ends for his own sake, more or less regardless of the needs of other persons or the consequence of his own acts. It is quite similar to the Freudian notion of the "id." In Freud, however, the id is nonmoral, the instinctive urge to get what we want when we want it; whereas in Paul the flesh has a definitely ethical connotation, for the flesh, or the fleshly (carnal) thinking *(phronema)*, is "enmity against God."[4]

The other idea embraced in the term flesh is heredity[5] in its biological sense but even more definitely in the sense of a damaging cultural pattern transmitted from one generation to the next. Flesh in this sense, as heredity, seems especially to imply any transmitted pattern of life in general or religion in particular which shuts God and His grace out of human life.

In the broadest sense, then, flesh with Paul stands for the motives, thoughts, attitudes, feelings, and emotions which one has "by nature." It is man when his chief end is to glorify himself and enjoy himself as long as possible in every possible way. It is what we have called Eros love, in action. And the damaging patterns of human relationships which it produces tend to be transmitted from parent to child unless the vicious sequence is broken.

Spirit is of a different order, not of "nature" but of God. We have already spoken of it enough to be able here to say briefly that Spirit is Agape love in action.

These two principles, or better, these two different kinds of love, contend against each other within the believer, Spirit "lusting" against flesh, and flesh "lusting" against Spirit.[6] The conflict between flesh and Spirit is further reflected by the inability of mind to control action by will, even though the transforming of mind has begun, for flesh still pulls in the old direction, impelling the believer to sin and perpetuating the inward war between flesh and Spirit.[7]

The struggle is lifelong. The famous passage in Romans 7 appears on its face to be autobiographical, in which case it is a mark of Paul's honesty in describing his own conflict after he became a Christian. If it is not autobiographical it can be taken as describing the experience of one who already has faith in Christ but still has deep conflict.[8] But if there is any doubt about the setting of this passage, Paul elsewhere unmistakably shows that he sees the conflict between flesh and Spirit as continuing in the believer.[9] And besides all these, the tenor of many, perhaps all, of the Pauline Epistles shows that he is writing to Christians who continue both to feel and to express the impulses of the flesh, whether or not Paul describes the conflict in terms of Spirit against flesh.[10]

The case of the Smith family illustrates better than abstract considerations usually do, that part of the concept of flesh which has to do with cultural heredity. In this instance it is possible to see a pattern of malignant human relationships passed along through three generations. But at the same time one can also feel the Spirit struggling to break the chain of malignant parent-child relationships. Both Arthur Smith and his son Alex are scenes of continuing conflict between flesh and Spirit in the Pauline sense. The success of the Spirit is not too brilliant in the body of Arthur, but there seems to be reasonable hope that Alex may be liberated into a much greater freedom than has been true of his father.

Against this background of continuing conflict, we are now to consider, in particular, how the healing of anxiety, the release of hostility, and the re-education of self-judgment are affected by the relationships within the Christian society.

THE HEALING OF ANXIETY

Parts of the doctrine of redemption have to do with the allaying of man's more basic anxiety, within a set of relationships where the meaning of God's redemptive Agape can be verbally stated in preaching and in pastoral counseling, and can also be lived in the feelings and emotions that characterize the actual human relationships.

The statements which the minister is entitled to make regarding God's acceptance and forgiveness are unmistakably designed to get at the deeper anxieties of any person who feels insecure and helpless in a vast universe. The assertions legitimately drawn from Christian theology are as sweeping as it is possible to make them. The great credal terms express a relatively small number of salient ideas, which are capable of unlimited variety, expansion, and depth of sincere feeling.

Some of the more prominent are such as these. God's love is ever actively reaching out to "seek and to save" any person who desires to have it so. Faith in Christ is the human condition of God's forgiveness. The death of Christ both accomplishes and guarantees forgiveness. God's forgiveness is complete, lacking in no respect whatever. Guilt as responsibility for sins that are past is held up to unflinching view and completely absolved in Christ. This holds for an individual's own personal past, and for any hereditary guilt which he may be regarded as sharing. Thus in those communions which carry the doctrine of original sin to its farthest extreme, complete removal of guilt as hereditary responsibility is always offered on the grounds of the death of Christ. The fact that such doctrines have often been questionable in exegesis and more dependent on man's logic than on God's revealed character, need not prevent one from recognizing the great importance of the two-sided thing they are seeking to express: that God's mercy is as wide and as deep as the sea of man's sin; and that no matter what a man or his ancestors have been, the slate is wiped clean when he believes into Christ. All the sin that has ever been in him is taken over by Christ, taken up to the Cross, and left there with God forever. In brief, the entire range of the consequences of sin is under view, and yet the most perfect forgiveness that can be expressed by human symbols is pledged to any man who repents and believes. Nothing that could be done by theology and its symbols to reassure anxious man of God's acceptance upon conditions man can fulfill, has been left undone.

And yet the verbal theology is not enough. Arthur Smith serves here to remind us that verbal theological reassurance even in preaching and pastoral conferences does not get to the bottom of a man's need. Indeed, the more urgent Smith's spiritual need becomes, the less can that need be met by merely *telling* him the truth about God's redemption. Precisely the same kind of thing holds also in the case of the son Alex, although not to so deep an extent. Both Arthur and his son required actual emotional acceptance by the minister and the congregation, if the verbal assertions of the church regarding forgiveness were to be made valid.

This acceptance of them as they are, met them; perhaps not perfectly—when is it ever so? But evidently the acceptance was genuine. That acceptance on the human side, by the Body of Christ, matches what is meant on the divine side by God's "justification" and puts at least a little of the "power of God" into human relations in a church. With the father, Arthur, perhaps the basic anxiety arising from his own earlier experience is too deep to be fully healed in this manner. Some of the episodes suggest that this is the case, as often it is in a congregation. In that event the minister alone is ordinarily not competent to be the agent of God for a complete healing of anxiety, and a psychiatrist may be needed who is able to work under better controlled conditions. But even so it is not to be overlooked that whatever his story, this man is back at his work, carrying on.

Anxiety seems to be deep in Alex also, and it may betray itself in other ways in the future. But it is entirely possible that the minister's own feelings as he so suggestively handled the episode of the stolen money, may have turned a tide which could easily have flowed toward delinquency with open aggression, or toward some form of destructive self-punishment. Alex's still unresolved anxiety may be reflected in the fact that when he attempts to break out of his father's domination, he is drawn to a religious career. Is this a temporary phase in the gaining of his freedom, or will it prove to be the career he desires when his freedom of choice is more complete? Here, also, only time will provide the answer.

But in thinking of redemption from anxiety, attention must not be so fixed upon the remedial functions of the Body of Christ as to make one overlook its constructive and preventive functions as far as anxiety is concerned. If malignant relationships are transmitted from one generation to the next, so are beneficent ones. In proportion as the church fulfills its mission in human society it will be constantly doing two things which help to pull human society away from the abyss into which "the flesh" would otherwise impel us. It will forever be breaking up old transmissible patterns of malignant relationships, not by means of external force, but by means of those internal revolutions effected when Agape transcends Eros. And it will be forever creating in human society new family units. In these, husband and wife embody as much of Agape love as they are capable of having in their relationship with each other in a fellowship of equals before God. From such unions ordinarily are born children relatively free from basic anxiety and therefore the less fettered emotionally as they begin life.

Into such families catastrophe will come as to others, for they are no more immune to wars, earthquakes, plague, and lightning, than their "unjust" neighbors are. But in so far as the members of that family are free from basic anxiety and have basic confidence in each other and in God, they go into a day of unexpected darkness with an inward light which will not long be dimmed.

THE RELEASE OF HOSTILITY

In earlier lectures it was repeatedly called to mind that hostility often underlies guilt, and that hostility itself is stirred when one is frustrated. There are many causes of frustration, of course, domination being one of them. Other things being equal we can expect that when a person is dominated by another, his hostility will be aroused; and if he cannot openly release his hostility, there may be a sense of guilt with symptoms of it cropping out. Accordingly we are to regard the symptoms of guilt within a religious society as possibly pointing to hostility arising out of the relationships in that society.

The case of the Smiths offers a tempting field for speculation at this point. Is hostility the underlying motif that runs from one generation to the next in this instance? Could the guilt symptoms of both father and son have been approached still more effectively if there had been better opportunity for the hostility to be released? We cannot know the answers to these questions in this instance, but generally in confronting guilt symptoms in a society, whether family or church, one may well ask such questions as, What is producing the hostility in the relationships? Can the underlying cause be altered? Can such hostility as is inevitably aroused in the course of individual growth be released, accepted, and turned to good account; or is the structure of the society such that all hostility has to be obscured, treated as if it did not exist, and perhaps repressed from conscious recognition by the one who feels the hostility?

The nature of this problem of hostility in the Christian society, whether it be family or church, is confused at the outset unless two things are kept in view. One is the fact that both family and church arouse hostility in their members as an unavoidable by-product of the relationships which produce growth. This we have already discussed in connection with family relationships, and if it is true in the family we must expect it to be so in the church as well. If hostility in some of its forms is an unavoidable phase of growing toward emotional maturity in Agape love, not all hostility is unwholesome from the psychological view, nor unmitigated evil from the spiritual point of view. We then have the problem in actual living of distinguishing between hostility which can be a prelude to growth, and hostility which is becoming destructive. This problem cannot be solved so long as the hostility is concealed and kept back from release.

The other fact to keep before ourselves is that Christianity, as often understood and lived, puts a tremendous pressure on its members to hide their own hostility from themselves as well as from others, and to deny that they have it at all. The constant verbal reiteration of the word "love," without opening up its meaning, and without a correspondingly frank facing of hatred, may be partly responsible for the mischief frequently wrought in those circles where Christians suppose they can transform the emotional life by means of exhortations as to the way "we ought to feel." When a Christian receives no encouragement to be honest about himself and his relationships, matters can be made yet worse by loading him with advice which he cannot follow and which often results in merely increasing his sense of guilt. The concealment of hostility thus puts a premium on hypocrisy by encouraging one of the deepest forms of dishonesty; assists one in putting a sanctimonious label upon a "temple of God" with rotten foundations; and piles up more and more guilt symptoms to make the relationships between members of a church still more distorted.

The force of all such considerations drives us to seek for avenues along which the hostility that is constantly coming up out of human relationships may be absorbed *in relationships* so as to become a prelude to further spiritual growth. For that purpose we may regard, first, the human relationships in the Body of Christ, then the relationship between the believer and God; after which it will be necessary to examine some of the moral problems involved in accepting hostility.

Authority Between Persons. The crux of the matter, as far as relationships between persons are concerned, seems to lie in the authority which one person assumes over another. In light of what is known of the effects of domination we may take it as probable that in family or church, the greater the extent of the authority exercised by one person or group over another person or group, the greater will be the hostility aroused in those dominated. The fact that the hostility is not open is likely to be very deceptive. The concealment of the hostility because of domineering authority may only hide the gathering storm which eventually may blow the authority to pieces, as happened to the Roman

Church at the Reformation; and as happens in a too strict family from which a youth runs away to gain the freedom denied him at home. But the gathering storm may be turned inward, remaining undetected but eventually becoming strong enough to destroy the persons who cannot release it.

It is notable, too, that when politically and economically dispossessed people seek or create a church, they so often turn to, or make, one which permits the individual common man to have a real voice in his own credal statements or church government. They may thus achieve a relatively more democratic society, as the Methodists did in drawing out of the Church of England. They may achieve an almost complete democracy as the Baptists have often done, and as the Disciples did in repudiating Presbyterianism. But those earnest men who argue for any one form of church government from Scriptural grounds would do well to consider also whether it may be a sign of God's providence that the Scriptural evidence on this point is not conclusive. They might also ask whether God designed it that we should learn something about church authority from the testimony of history as well as the testimony of Scripture.

But in the last analysis the degree of domination is better measured by the actual relationships that exist between the persons concerned, than it is by the formal pattern of authority in family or church. What is required in these relationships is at least fourfold.

One is that the relationships in the church be such as steadily to press the responsibility for decisions in matters of ethical conduct back upon the individual. The constant temptation of the minister and the lay worker in the church is to assume this responsibility on behalf of the spiritually less mature, and then try to persuade them to act accordingly. The temptation is increased whenever perplexed persons say, "Tell us what to do!" All who are accustomed to live by regimen and schedule at home, in school, in church work, in business, or wherever else, become tempters to the churchman here, luring him on to ascend a mountain of spiritual authority and hand down the Christian "law" to what he thinks is a people hungry for his leadership in morals. What he does not see is that in so responding he has pointed them back toward wandering a little longer under a well-meant spiritual dictatorship.

It is precisely this from which the New Testament is seeking to set men free in matters of ethics. There the multitudinous details of the Jewish law as a predetermined code of ethics and an unbearable burden upon conscience are abolished, not in order to free men from obligation to their fellows, but as a way of making "love in action" possible. In its stead is enunciated the one law of love, and the believer is made responsible for discovering what it means and putting it into action. There can be no code of love; such is a contradiction in terms. There can only be the most powerful of all suggestion: the life of One who lived it perfectly Himself and whose Spirit comes into those who confess Him Lord. It was a frightening responsibility for persons who had grown up by rule, and a heady one for those who supposed liberty meant license. But if they were to be truly free in the Spirit, there was no substitute, and any sly return to living by a code could but deliver them back to bondage.

But it must be understood that when responsibility for decisions is pressed back upon the individual, his anxiety and his hostility are likely to be aroused. This is a part of the pain of growing up. Since the problem of accepting hostility is involved we shall return to the subject below.

A second necessity is that we admit the right of persons to take part genuinely in reaching decisions affecting the entire group, whether as a congregation, a denomination, or a still larger group. When this is disregarded, the structure of the society becomes top-heavy with authority and decisions are reached without common consent. The arrogating of spiritual authority over one's fellow Christians, under the guise of alleged spiritual sanctions, is a subtle process in the church. It can go on until there is no limit in heaven, or purgatory, or hell, upon the pretensions of the church to control the destiny of men. It can go a lesser distance in the same direction, until ecclesiastics, declaring themselves spokesmen for God, thwart the desires of common men for a world Christianity, the constitutional structure of whose Body will make unity among Christians a reality. It can go on under the guise of administration instead of polity, until churchmen in administrative posts defeat the desire of common Christians in small communities to be one in Christ as an actual congregation. These and many other instances of their kind have aroused hostility which the lay Christian finds it hard to understand in himself, until he begins to ask whether perhaps it is *he* and not the ecclesiastics who is hearing the voice of the Spirit.

When hostility is stirred in a religious society by autocratic leadership a sort of underground resistance begins to develop. This resistance is a familiar phenomenon in response to many kinds of proposals which emanate from overhead. For example, proposals looking toward church unity, when reached without rather general consent, may encounter strenuous opposition from those who are asked to enter a union. But almost the exact reverse may also be true; there may be a widespread desire for a certain union which is blocked by men who assume to speak for the people, when in reality they are only increasing the desire of common people to be rid of a leadership which is not responsive to the common will.

Again, this phenomenon of underground resistance is familiar in connection with programs of church work which are planned in offices remote from actual congregations and must be "sold" to the people as a manufacturer might attempt to do with high-pressure methods. The entire program of church work, designed to increase efficiency, then tends to become mere propaganda. The Christian society becomes a place where one can exhibit that quiet hostility which consists in refraining from action in matters where he has no voice. But in so doing he is left open to the charge of disloyalty, and may be soundly browbeaten by his leaders for his indifference, and made to feel guilty for what essentially is another man's sin.

But as common people begin to understand that neither the authority nor the wisdom of God is confined to bishops, ministers, professors in theological schools, and administrative heads of church affairs, they still lack means for reconstructing the church in response to the Spirit, without rebellions and schisms. Lacking those means, Christianity often has to renew itself by springing up afresh from the soil of common life. The growth and vigor of what we like to call the emotional sects and the fanatical forms of Christianity *may* mean, among other things, that the Spirit of Christ in our day is creating new types of relationships within the Body of Christ, perhaps to the end that the more rigid forms of Christianity shall be displaced and die.

But this suicide need not be. Evidently a new strategy is required in Protestantism for the purpose of thrusting back upon local congregations the responsibility for deliberation, decision, and action, instead of the responsibility for either adopting or combating a ready-made solution handed down to them. We have unrivalled opportunity in the denominations to check the great drift toward unthinking mass action by restoring the right and duty of deliberative, constructive action to smaller, face-to-face groups in local congregations.

A third requirement is that we admit the right of the individual to dissent intellectually from the majority in matters of belief, without necessarily being charged with heresy, and without having to find his Christian fellowship by withdrawing to another denomination whose creed will coincide perfectly with his own. The denial of this right has produced hostility among Christians whose effects defy all calculation. The acceptance of it involves still other problems of equal magnitude, for if carried far enough this right will result in the complete disappearance of the Christian society. But it can hardly be doubted that in the interest of intellectual conviction the Body of Christ has already rent itself to fragments, and unless it can turn its path toward faith in Christ, instead of faith in theology or faith in itself as a church, it holds promise of dying by its own hand, which once more is a sign of our own hostility and guilt.

A fourth is that we admit into actual relationships within the Body of Christ the principle enunciated in the classic saying, "For as many of you as have been baptized into Christ have put on Christ. There is neither Jew nor Greek, there is neither bond nor free, there is neither male nor female: for ye are all one in Christ Jesus."[11] Here is recognition of the fact that "in the world" there *are* strata of society with mutual hostility due to differences of race, of social and economic status, and of sex. And there is the revolutionary insight that in as many as have been truly baptized into Christ, these differences are lost in oneness in Christ Jesus.

Is this principle designed to transform even our habitual thinking—our *phren*—concerning superiority, inferiority, and domination, as between races, colors, classes, and sexes? What else, indeed, *could* be the meaning? But it is to be noted well that this oneness is *in the Body of Christ,* that is, between the members of actual churches. It is not a text for a general crusade as touching race relations, class conflict, or feminism. Movements for such purposes have their function. But by such means we can take refuge in forming societies for the preventing of this or that, passing impressive resolutions, and then going home to live as we were. Of many meetings for such purposes it might be said as Paul did, "They who seemed to be somewhat in conference added nothing to me."[12]

This is, rather, the goading Spirit of Christ, seeking to get into the *phren* of our actual emotional relationships within the Body of Christ; seeking, moreover, to penetrate into the persons on both sides of a hereditary barrier, and reconcile them into one. But as long as the domination of race over race, class over class, or sex over sex, continues in any respect within the church, so long is the church a breeding ground of those very antagonisms which have already shattered society and will continue so to do until the Spirit can find a society ready not merely to proclaim some new "Atlantic Charter," but to put it to work without sidestepping.

That society can be the church if the members of *actual churches* have the courage to make it so. For such an end was the church born, as witness the struggle which emerged so early over taking the gospel to the Gentiles, and then eating with them on terms of genuine fellowship between equals. But the birth pains of a regenerated church are hard, for this kind of rebirth means no less than giving up to death some of the fleshly motives of superiority, and raising to life those new motives which can flourish only in a fellowship of genuine equals before God.

Honesty with God. In the relationship with God as well as in the relationship with one's fellow believers, there is opportunity for the release of hostility. Prayer, which is fellowship with God, is the channel for its recognition and release.

The private prayer of confession is an unexcelled time, in the believer's relationship with God, for honesty in the recognition of such antagonisms and hatreds as one is capable of understanding in himself. It surely will not need to be said that this is not a matter of praying against the "enemy" within one's household, or among his acquaintances, or his competitor, whether near at hand or beyond the sea. It is rather a matter of being honest enough to face one's own hostility in the presence of God, with all pretenses stripped away.

Perhaps the last refuge of a Christian's despair is his attempt to hide from God a hostility to the will of God as that will is revealed by the course of events in individual and general history. A man may loathe God because of some event that has befallen a loved one, or because a human plan has failed, or because disaster overtakes church or world. But which is better: the subterfuge of verbally hiding that hostility during prayer and mentally pretending to a love and resignation he in no wise feels; or such confidence in God as will dare to believe that God would welcome our saying what, in fact, *is* in our hearts? Into which of these is it more likely that the peace of God, as well as the grace of God, can eventually come?

The Acceptance of Hostility. As we have now pointed out, hostility is constantly being produced in the Christian society, and keeping that society truly democratic provides no insurance against the arousal of hostility. But the more nearly the Christian society approaches being a fellowship of persons who are genuine equals before God, the more likely is it that the hostility can be accepted as it arises, and thus be kept from gathering a strength which later may become either outwardly explosive or inwardly destructive.

But what is involved in "accepting hostility"? Some examples of the relationships in which it arises and in which it needs to be accepted as it arises may be taken. One is in the relationship between the minister and some person who has come to odds with society through infringing the moral code. If such a person seeks the minister, the latter may encounter hostility toward himself at the beginning of this particular relationship. That barrier in the relationship will have to be transcended by his acceptance of the hostility toward himself before he can hope to become an active and effective agent of God in the redemption of this individual from guilt. The hostility from the offender toward the minister, and the minister's acceptance of it, are illustrated in this incident.

A group of young ministers sat around a table with Fred, who had stolen several automobiles, been in reform school, and was now approaching his return to freedom. He had agreed to come and talk with them on the question of what a minister could do to help a boy who is in trouble.

Fred had said, "You've got to know what it is to be in jail, and not have a friend, and have everybody down on you."

One of the young men, Mr. R, asked, "Fred, some of us haven't been in *this* kind of trouble and we don't know what it feels like. How can we get to know how it feels?"

Instantly Fred rose to his feet. His voice grew hard, as he pointed a finger and shot out the words: "It might do you good to steal a car and get in jail, and *then* you'd know what it's like." The air fairly crackled as he spoke.

Mr. R replied thoughtfully, and with no trace of antagonism in response, "I guess it does seem to you that we don't know what it feels like."

In those few seconds, there had been a small explosion of a trapped boy's hostility toward "the good man" who seemed to threaten for a moment to become his judge. But the young man had accepted the hostility, had assumed no self-righteous air in his reply, and the hostility in Fred apparently subsided as quickly as it had flamed out. They were then ready for the next step in a shared journey as comrades seeking a way out, and not as enemies arrayed against each other.

Again, anxiety and hostility are likely to be aroused in the person who seeks specific advice on a problem in living, and has the responsibility put back in his own lap. The minister who understands this hostility as a phase of growing out of spiritual dependency into spiritual responsibility, is better able to accept it without responding in kind and thus letting matters degenerate into argument. It has been said that the rapport is the anesthetic for the operation of exposing anxiety and hostility.

If these two kinds of hostility, that toward the professional good man and that toward one who will not become the taker of his responsibility, can be accepted, the minister may find that much more malignant hostilities begin to come out; such as that of wife toward husband, child to parent, and so on. It may be found that some such hostility underlies stealing, sex delinquencies, drinking, and a great array of other guilt outcroppings. But what then? Can the minister accept these profounder hatreds without turning into a lecturer on morals, there in the privacy of the interview?

His theology is pertinent here if he can really take it into his own emotions. Exactly the same question confronts him as confronted the first Christians. Justification by faith, as we have shown, was the formula reached. But good men were afraid of that doctrine. When they heard the proposal that a sinful man would be accepted by a just God as righteous on the ground of nothing more than *faith* in Christ, they were scandalized, avowing that this teaching meant nothing more than letting down the moral bars so that sin might abound. What they failed to see was that in no other way than by a change in the feelings and emotions could a compromise with moral standards be *avoided*. Only then can love begin to grow in a sinful man, and his old, destructive emotions be drained off into the cleansing sea of God's forgiveness.

When these deeper hatreds begin to be brought out, then, the minister faces not only a crisis in the man with whom he talks, but one in himself also. Can he have so much of God in him as to accept what is brought out of the deeper recesses, without horror, without blaming, without preachments; confident that if *he* can accept it, he will thereby validate the promises of the Almighty?

If this much is done, mutual hostility between the offender and the congregation is still to be faced. Admit that some barriers to complete redemption, of this kind, may never be completely surmounted. Nevertheless a congregation often is quick to sense the great human drama of death and resurrection which is being lived out in the midst of them, and are eager to have a share in it. The congregation of which the Smiths are members is evidence.

And so is a small congregation in the town of X, where a girl of the community, unmarried, had just borne a child. Space will not allow recounting what transpired between the minister and the young mother, but a day came shortly when the young woman, who still had no husband, stood holding her infant, as the two awaited baptism before the congregation in an atmosphere that spoke acceptance of mother and child as no words alone could ever do. Most of what might have been said was left unsaid, and it was better so. But as the young mother made her simple confession of faith in Christ that day, the people understood that both she and her babe had found in the church a homeland.

There is many another form of hostility to which not even a reference can be made here. What has been said must serve as samples out of the vast torrent of hostility itself and its related outlets; and must serve, moreover, as reminders that genuine accept-

ance by the Body of Christ of the man, as he now is, is a prelude to
sharing with him in becoming what he may be.

THE RE-EDUCATION OF SELF-JUDGMENT

In order that the believer's liberty may be complete, one thing
more is wanting: that he should accept himself for what he is, to
match the acceptance given him by God and accorded him in the
society of Christian believers.

This is hardly less a miracle than that he should have the other
two—acceptance by God and his fellows. Yet to the achieving of this
final liberation of conscience the New Testament addresses itself
with no less thoroughness than in the case of the other two. A believer in Christ has been set free from condemnation: then let him
so regard himself, and accept in his own estimate of himself what
has been pledged by the Lord God. Two great doctrines have direct
bearing on this liberation of the believer from self-condemnation.

Of these, one is the doctrine of election. When put in terms of
strict logic and thus abstracted from human relationships it has
sometimes been made repellent to reason or abhorrent to feeling.
But in its setting, as shown in Romans, it is the final anchor of hope
for any man who believes in Christ, earnestly tries to live by the
Spirit, and then sensing as never before his own imperfection, is
tempted to ask, "Am I any more than a wishful thinker; after all
Christ has done, am I a castaway because of what I have done?"
For such a man the seal of God is set upon his hopes by the hymn
of final victory:

What shall we then say to these things? If God be for us [as he is],
who can be against us? He that spared not his own Son, but delivered him up for us all, how shall he not with him also freely give
us all things? Who shall lay any thing to the charge of God's elect?
It is God that justifieth. Who is he that condemneth? It is Christ
that died, yea rather, that is risen again, who is even at the right

hand of God, who also maketh intercession for us. Who shall separate us from the love of Christ? shall tribulation, or distress, or per-
secution, or famine, or nakedness, or peril, or sword? . . . Nay, in
all these things we are more than conquerors through him that loved
us. For I am persuaded, that neither death, nor life, nor angels, nor
principalities, nor powers, nor things present, nor things to come,
nor height, nor depth, nor any other creature, shall be able to
separate us from the love of God, which is in Christ Jesus our
Lord.[13]

A second element in the New Testament which bears directly
upon the believer's judgment of himself is the doctrine of conscience. The gist of that teaching in its negative aspect is that a
man's moral estimate of himself is thoroughly undependable until
it becomes *conscience* in the sense suggested by the etymology of
the word both in English and in Greek: *con*-science, a knowledge or
estimate of the self in keeping with the appraisal of that self by the
God, that is, the Spirit, within the believer's self.

Two states of conscience, therefore, are treacherous because they
register unjust appraisals. The one is the approving conscience of
the good man who prides himself upon his own virtues; the other,
the disapproving conscience of the believer who condemns and
punishes himself for his own sin. The former is the conscience of the
pagan or the hypocrite whose judgment upon himself is not God's
judgment upon him.[14] The latter is the weak conscience of one who
does not dare to take the final venture of faith and let his own judgment upon himself coincide with God's acceptance of him as justified in Christ, and who therefore is afraid to act with true freedom.[15]

On its positive side the doctrine of conscience points to the highest
function of self-consciousness which a human being is capable of
exercising. The act of self-judgment of one who is in Christ, as pic-
tured by the word itself and by the usage of that word, is almost in-
conceivably bold. It is as if a judgment scene were transpiring con-

stantly. The believer's self is the object of judgment. There is a judgment seat shared both by the self, who is the object of the judgment, and by God Himself. The two, God and the believer, have, as it were, a co-consciousness. They give judgment upon the believer. And as a result of that co-consciousness with God, a believer in Christ is able to make so incredible a statement as this:

With me it is a very small thing that I should be judged of you, or of man's judgment: yea, I judge not mine own self. For I know nothing by myself [or more accurately, I know nothing *against* myself; i. e., my self-consciousness here does not function by itself but is shared with God]; yet am I not hereby justified: but he that judgeth me is the Lord.[16]

As in the case of the healing of anxiety and the release of hostility, so with conscience. It requires to be exercised in a body of relationships where the right to conscience is not merely yielded, but is thrust upon the believer. The church is, or is designed to be, such a society. In proportion as it fulfills its redemptive mission it becomes a training ground for liberating the conscience *from* bondage to external codes and social pressures, and liberating it *into* the widest freedom in the universe, which is freedom to be on God's side in the lifelong, agelong conflict between the flesh and the Spirit. Such a man is justified by faith. Let him come into a peace with God, through Jesus Christ; a peace which cannot be taken away by the vicissitudes of life nor by the incident of death.

"Therefore being justified by faith, let us have peace with God through our Lord Jesus Christ."[17]

NOTES

Chapter I

1 Goethe, *Faust*, Part One; p. 37 of edition by A. L. Burt, translated by Anne Swanwick.

2 Chekov, *The Cherry Orchard*, p. 92.

3 Heidel, Alexander, *The Babylonian Genesis* (Chicago, 1942).

4 Hopkins, E. W., *The Religions of India*, p. 40f (Boston, 1902).

5 *Ibid.*, p. 186f.

6 Swanton, J. R., in Bureau of American Ethnology, Bulletin 103, p. 197 (Washington, 1921).

7 Bureau of American Ethnology, Bulletin 135, p. 1 (Washington, 1942).

8 Swanton, J. R., in Bureau of American Ethnology, Bulletin 43, p. 168f (Washington, 1911).

9 Valliant, G. C., *Aztecs of Mexico*, p. 177f (New York, 1941).

10 Barton, G. A., *Religions of the World*, p. 204 (Chicago, 1917); Werner, E. T. C., *Dictionary of Chinese Mythology*, p. 593 (Shanghai, 1932); Ferguson, J. C., *Mythology of All Races*, p. 136f (Boston, 1928).

11 Moore, G. F., *History of Religions*, p. 381f (New York, 1914).

12 Hesiod, *Theogony*, 1, 115f.

13 Haigh, A. E., *The Tragic Drama of the Greeks*, p. 5f (Oxford, 1896); McDougall, Wm., "The Rival Schools of Psychology," *The Register*, XVIII, No. 3, July-September, 1929 (Louisville Presbyterian Seminary, Louisville, Kentucky).

14 As in Euripides, *Iphigenia in Aulis*.

15 As in Aeschylus, *Agamemnon*.

16 As in Aeschylus, *Choephoroe*.

17 As in Aeschylus, *Eumenides*.

18 Sophocles, *Oedipus, King of Thebes; Oedipus at Colonus*.

19 Haigh, *op. cit.*, p. 86f., 171f., 261f.

20 *Republic*, VI.

21 *Phaedo*, e. g., 66f.

22 *Phaedrus*, 248-253.

23 McDougall, *op. cit.;* Ueberweg, F., *History of Philosophy,* translated by G. S. Morris, Vol. I, p. 169f (New York, 1896); Pillsbury, W. B., *The History of Psychology,* p. 24f (New York, 1929); Case, T., "Aristotle," *Encyc. Brit.,* 11th ed., esp. p. 512f.; Burton, E. D., *Spirit, Soul, and Flesh,* p. 41f (Chicago, 1918).

24 Ueberweg, *op. cit.,* Vol. I, p. 185f., Marcus Aurelius, *Meditations.*

25 Murray, G., *The Stoic Philosophy* (London, 1915); cf., especially p. 53f.

26 Hopkins, *op. cit.,* p. 305f.

Chapter II

1 Kant, *Critique of Pure Reason,* translated by J. M. D. Meikeljohn, p. 35 (New York, 1900).

2 For details see, e. g., Pillsbury, *op. cit.*

3 Hegel, *Philosophy of History,* translated by J. Sibree, pp. 60-87 (New York, 1900).

4 Deutsch, H., *The Mentally Ill in America,* p. 88f., 158f (New York, 1937).

5 Schopenhauer, *The World as Will and Idea.*

6 Rank, O., *Beyond Psychology,* especially p. 173f (Camden, N. J., 1941).

7 Jung, C. G., *Psychological Types* (New York, 1926).

8 The two streams which we have here called "academic psychology" and "depth psychology" are virtually the same as those called "Lockian psychology" and "Leibnitzian psychology" by Gordon W. Allport in his book *Becoming* (New Haven, 1955). This book contains a brilliant critique of the two streams.

9 It must be said that statements in this paragraph regarding the ethical implications of psychoanalysis are open to challenge. An orthodox Freudian would probably insist that the kind of development which psychoanalysis furthers *is* maturity. Nevertheless whenever man's obligation to himself is so elevated as to become the primary goal of human striving, the resulting problems in social ethics seem to become insoluble. See, e.g., Erich Fromm's effort to develop a "psychology of ethics" in his book *Man for Himself* (New York, 1947).

Chapter III

1 *King Lear*, Act I, Sc. 2.

2 Karpman, B., "Criteria for Knowing Right from Wrong," *Journal of Criminal Psychotherapy*, II, pp. 376-86 (January, 1941).

3 Mullen, J. G., *Psychological Factors in the Pastoral Treatment of Scruples* (Baltimore, 1927).

4 Cannon, W. B., *Bodily Changes in Pain, Hunger, Fear, and Rage*, Part I (Boston, 1915).
   Henry, G. W., *Essentials of Psychiatry*, Ch. 1 (Baltimore, 1931).

5 Jones, E., "Fear, Guilt, and Hate," *International Journal of Psychoanalysis*, X, pp. 383-397 (London, 1929).

6 Levy, D. M., *Studies in Sibling Rivalry* (American Orthopsychiatric Association, 1937).

7 Preu, P. W., "The Concept of Psychopathic Personality," in Hunt, McV. (ed.), *Personality and the Behavior Disorders* (New York, 1944).

8 Szurek, S. A., "Notes on the Genesis of Psychopathic Personality Trends," *Psychiatry*, V, No. 1, pp. 1-6 (February, 1942).

Chapter IV

1 Noyes, A. P., *Modern Clinical Psychiatry*, p. 120 (Philadelphia, 1934).

2 Cf.,Horney, K., *The Neurotic Personality of Our Time*, p. 63 (New York, 1937).

3 Nygren, A., *Agape and Eros*, 2 Vols. (London, 1938).

4 Rank, O., *Beyond Psychology*, p. 173f (Camden, N. J., 1941).

5 Horney, *op. cit.*, p. 79 f.

6 Kierkegaard, S., *The Sickness Unto Death*, p. 17 f. (Princeton, 1941).

7 Niebuhr, Reinhold, *The Nature and Destiny of Man*, Vol. I, p. 178 f. (New York, 1941). See also his *The Self and the Dramas of History*, Chapter 4 (New York, 1955).

8 The principal works referred to are: Tillich, P., *The Courage to Be* (New Haven, 1952); May, Rollo, *The Meaning of Anxiety* (New York, 1950); Oates, W. E., *Anxiety in Christian Experience* (Philadelphia, 1955); and Stinnette, C. R., Jr., *Anxiety and Faith* (Greenwich, Conn., 1955). See

also Roberts, David E., *Psychotherapy and a Christian View of Man* (New York, 1950); and Outler, A. C., *Psychotherapy and the Christian Message* (New York, 1954).

9 Nunberg, H., "The Feeling of Guilt," *Psychoanalytic Quarterly*, III, pp. 589-604, 1934.

10 Zilborg, G., "Sidelights on Parent-Child Antagonism," *American Journal of Orthopsychiatry*, II, pp. 35-43 (January, 1932).

11 Sullivan, H. S., in Kasanin, J. S. (ed.) *Language and Thought in Schizophrenia*, p. 4f (Los Angeles, 1944).

12 Wendell, B., *Cotton Mather, the Puritan Priest* (New York, 1891); Nevins, W. S., *Witchcraft in Salem Village* (Boston, 1892).

13 Lampl, H., "Contribution to case histories: a case of borrowed guilt," *International Journal of Psychoanalysis*, VIII, pp. 143-158 (April, 1927).

14 Levin, M., "The Feeling of Guilt and Its Effects," *Mental Hygiene*, XV, p. 724f (October, 1931).

15 Menninger, K., *Man Against Himself*, p. 87f (New York, 1938).

16 Lipton, S., "Dissociated Personality," *Psychiatric Quarterly*, XVII, pp. 35-56 (January, 1943).

17 Boisen, A. T., *The Exploration of the Inner World*, p. 15f (Chicago, 1930).

Chapter V

1 Ackerly, S., "Rebellion and Its Relation to Delinquency and Neurosis in Sixty Adolescents," *The American Journal of Orthopsychiatry*, III, pp. 147-160.

2 Jung, C. G., *Modern Man in Search of a Soul*, pp. 39-40 (New York, 1933). Used with permission of Harcourt, Brace & Company.

3 Cf., e. g., Rank, *op. cit.*

Taft, J., *The Dynamics of Therapy* (New York, 1933).

Healy, W., and Bronner, A. F., *New Light on Delinquency and Its Treatment* (New Haven, 1936).

Karpf, F. B., *Dynamic Relationship Therapy*, p. 20f (Los Angeles, 1939).

Allen, F. H., *Psychotherapy with Children* (New York, 1942).

Chapter VI

1 Luke 11:50.

2 Romans 3:19.

3 John 1:1.

4 Cf., e. g., Colossians, where Inge remarks that all the elements of the Logos doctrine appear under a slightly different vocabulary.

5 Luke 1:78.

6 Sherrill, L. J., *The Rise of Christian Education,* Chap. IV (New York, 1944)

7 Luke 4:18, 19.

8 Matthew 4:24.

9 Mark 5:22-24.

10 Leviticus 14:34-53.

11 Matthew 4:24.

12 Matthew 17:15.

13 Luke 11:20.

14 John 5:8; Mark 2:9 (which is another incident almost identical in wording).

15 Luke 6:10.

16 Luke 7:50.

17 Luke 17:19.

18 Matthew 9:29.

19 Matthew 15:28.

20 Chamberlain, W. D., *The Meaning of Repentance,* pp. 222-223 (Philadelphia, 1943). Used by permission of The Westminster Press.

21 E. g., John 3:16.

22 Sherrill, L. J., *op. cit.,* p. 141f.

23 Romans 2:14, 15.

24 Acts 16:31 specifically; many other equivalent expressions occur in Acts.

25 Galatians 2:16; 2:20; 3:22; Philippians 3:9.

26 Colossians 1:4.

27 Galatians 2:16; Philippians 1:29; John 3:16; 14:1.

28 Acts 11:17; 16:31.

29 Matthew 23:13.

Chapter VII

[1] These subjects, for example, are treated in: Burton, E. D., *Spirit, Soul, and Flesh* (Chicago, 1918); Robinson, H. W., *The Christian Experience of the Holy Spirit* (New York, 1928); and Robinson, H. W., *The Old Testament, Its Making and Meaning* (Nashville, 1937).

[2] Psalms 1:4.

[3] II Kings 3:17.

[4] II Samuel 22:11.

[5] Ezekiel 37:9, 10.

[6] II Kings 2:16.

[7] I Samuel 18:10.

[8] Judges 15:14.

[9] I Samuel 10:6, 10.

[10] Judges 3:10.

[11] Judges 6:34.

[12] Exodus 31:3.

[13] Isaiah 48:16.

[14] Isaiah 61:1.

[15] Ezekiel 3:12.

[16] Ezekiel 3:14.

[17] Ezekiel 11:5.

[18] Ezekiel 2:2.

[19] Ezekiel 37:4, 10.

[20] Genesis 2:7.

[21] Leviticus 17:11 (A.S.V. margin).

[22] Genesis 2:7.

[23] Job 27:3.

[24] Isaiah 65:5.

[25] II Samuel 22:9; Psalms 18:15.

[26] Job 4:9.

[27] Job 30:27.

[28] Jeremiah 31:20.

[29] Psalms 22:14.

[30] Lamentations 1:20.

[31] Canticles 5:4.

[32] Genesis 43:30.

83 I Kings 3:26.
34 Isaiah 1:2-4.
85 Rank, O., *Beyond Psychology*, p. 117f., p. 280f (Camden, 1941).
36 Acts 2:2.
37 Acts 2:3, 4.
38 Ephesians 2:8.
39 Cf. Acts 19:2, for the negative aspect of this point.
40 Galatians 4:6.
41 II Corinthians 3:17.
42 Acts 18:9; 23:11.
43 Philippians 2:5-11.
44 John 1:3.
45 Colossians 1:16, 17.
46 Galatians 6:15; Cf. II Corinthians 5:17 (A. S. V. margin in both passages).
47 Galatians 5:6.
48 Matthew 25:34-46.
49 Romans 8:9.
50 II Corinthians 3:17.
51 For example, in Matthew 10:28, man is not able to kill the soul, but the soul can be destroyed in hell. Passages such as I Peter 1:9; James 1:21; James 5:20, etc., suggest a soul futuristically saved apart from a body, but perhaps only because we are so accustomed to Platonic views of "soul" as to find it hard to translate *psyche* by "life."
52 Mark 8:34-38.
53 Romans 8:23.
54 Romans 11:3; 16:4; I Corinthians 15:45; II Corinthians 12:15 (A. S. V.); Philippians 2:30; I Thessalonians 2:8.
55 Romans 13:1; II Corinthians 1:23; Ephesians 6:6 (A. S. V. margin); Colossians 3:23 (A. S. V. margin).
56 Romans 2:9; Romans 13:1.
57 Luke 2:35.
58 Ephesians 6:6 and Colossians 3:23 may be understood as using "soul" to refer to a living being with strong feelings.
59 Philippians 1:27; A. V. "with one mind" is literally "with one soul."
60 I Thessalonians 5:23.

[61] In the thirteen epistles traditionally attributed to Paul, the word does not even appear in six of them, Galatians, II Thessalonians, I Timothy, II Timothy, Titus, and Philemon. In the remaining seven, the word is used only thirteen times.

[62] Romans 7:15-25.

[63] Romans 1:20; Ephesians 3:30.

[64] Titus 1:16.

[65] Romans 1:21; Galatians 4:9.

[66] Romans 1:28; 10:2.

[67] II Corinthians 3:14; 4:4.

[68] II Timothy 3:8.

[69] I Corinthians 14:20.

[70] Romans 12:3; Philippians 1:7.

[71] Romans 8:6.

[72] Romans 1:24.

[73] Romans 2:14, 15.

[74] Romans 10:9, 10.

[75] Romans 2:29.

[76] Romans 6:17.

[77] Romans 10:10; Ephesians 3:17; 6:5; II Thessalonians 3:5; II Timothy 2:22. The point is also illustrated from slightly different angles in Romans 2:5; 8:27; I Corinthians 2:9; II Corinthians 1:22; 3:3; 4:6; 5:12.

[78] II Corinthians 6:12; 7:15; Philippians 1:8; 2:1; Colossians 3:12; Philemon vss. 7, 12, 20.

[79] II Corinthians 6:12.

[80] I Corinthians 12:12f.

[81] Romans 12:4.

[82] Colossians 3:5.

[83] Romans 7:23.

[84] Romans 7:5.

[85] Galatians 5:19-21.

[86] Romans 15:30 (A. S. V.).

[87] Romans 10:17; Galatians 3:2, 5.

[88] I Corinthians 2:16; Ephesians 4:23; similarly, with the *nous* man may resist, cf. II Timothy 3:8.

89 This seems to be the general meaning in Romans 8:5; Philippians 2:5; 3:15; Romans 8:7-9; 8:27.
90 Romans 10:13-17.
91 I Corinthians 2:11; II Corinthians 7:1; Ephesians 2:2.
92 Cf. I Corinthians 15:45.
93 Romans 12:1.
94 Philippians 1:20.
95 I Corinthians 15:35-57.
96 I Corinthians 15:44-51. For the force of the argument the entire chapter must be read.
97 Romans 12:1, 2; Ephesians 4:23.
98 Romans 8:5, 6.
99 Galatians 4:6.
100 Ephesians 3:17.
101 II Corinthians 4:6.
102 Romans 5:5.
103 Colossians 3:15.
104 Ephesians 1:18.
105 II Corinthians 1:22.
106 Romans 6:13, 19.
107 Often; e. g., Romans 12:5; I Corinthians 6:15.
108 Philippians 1:8.
109 Cf. Philippians 2:1; Colossians 3:12; II Corinthians 7:15; Philemon vss. 7, 12, 20.
110 Matthew 23:37.
111 This has nothing in common with the view cautiously suggested by William James, that divine revolutionizing power may enter human personality through the "subconscious"; nor with that of C. G. Jung for whom "the racial unconscious" is God. The first pushes the problem behind a screen, the second equates God with the blind strivings of unrational Nature. Here God as personalized Spirit enters "the mind," that is, by mental processes of which we have some knowledge; but then as Personality and within the limits of our emotional assent, invades the depths of human personality, rational mind, attitudes, affections, "unconscious," and all.

[112] Quoted in Otto, R., *Idea of the Holy*, p. 38 (London, 1928).

[113] Many bad essays on good themes such as academic freedom, unfettered research, etc., have been tortured out of John 8:32 ("And ye shall know the truth, and the truth shall make you free"). The truth here is a Person, who can be known by experience (*ginosko*) as in John 14:6 ("I am the way, the truth, and the life").

[114] I Corinthians 15.

[115] Romans 6:4; Cf. also Romans 7:6.

[116] Romans 6:1-11.

Chapter VIII

[1] I John 3:9.

[2] I John 1:8-10; 2:1f. helps to resolve the problem of interpretation by further showing that John thinks of the believer as continuing to sin. If III John is from the same writer as I John, the evidence of his own hostility toward a fellow Christian, Diotrephes, is significant.

[3] I John 4:18.

[4] Romans 8:7. Also Romans 7:18, "In me (that is, in my flesh), dwelleth no good thing."

[5] In Galatians 4:21f., "flesh" stands for Judaism and "bondage"; while "Spirit" stands for Christ and liberation. In Philippians 3, "flesh" stands for Paul's own religious and cultural heritage as a strict Pharisee.

[6] Galatians 5:17.

[7] Romans 7:15-25.

[8] The preceding chapter in Romans has developed the theme of the believer's death and resurrection with Christ. Then in Chapter 7 comes the theme of conflict.

[9] Galatians 3:2f.; perhaps Galatians 5:16f. In I Corinthians 3:1f., "babes in Christ" are not yet "spiritual" but still are carnal; yet these have "believed," and are "temples of God," "holy," etc.

[10] Philippians 2:1-13; the conflict of the believers is between two kinds of habitual thinking (*phroneo*) which roughly equate with flesh and spirit. In I Corinthians the conflict is between what could be called a *"fleshly* Spirit," and a *"spiritual* Spirit." Earlier stages in Paul's thinking may be represented in the Thessalonian Epistles. In I Thessalonians 4 and 5, the

conflict is between light and darkness; the resurrection seems identified with light, and both these are associated with Christ's return. In II Thessalonians the conflict, still more internalized, is between God and the mysterious "man of sin," and God takes flaming vengeance on those who do not believe. The contrast between the conceptions of resurrection in I Thessalonians 4 and 5, and I Corinthians 15, is great, suggesting that if both are genuinely Pauline, his doctrine of redemption had developed far in a relatively brief time.

[11] Galatians 3:27, 28.

[12] Galatians 2:6.

[13] Romans 8:31-35, 37-39.

[14] Cf. Romans 2:15; Titus 1:15; I Timothy 4:2. The word conscience does not appear in the Gospels, but the equivalent of the hypocritical conscience is abundant there.

[15] I Corinthians 8:7, 10-12.

[16] I Corinthians 4:3, 4; in this general sense of shared self-consciousness, the word "conscience" is used many times. E. g., Acts 23:1; Romans 9:1; II Corinthians 1:12; I Timothy 1:5; 1:19; 3:9; II Timothy 1:3; Hebrews 9:9; 9:14; 10:2; 10:22; 13:18; I Peter 2:19; 3:16; 3:21.

[17] Romans 5:1 (A. S. V. margin).